LEARN ABOUT

Life Force Energy

FROM A MASTER

MARY BANNON

Learn About Life Force Energy From A Master

ISBN-978-1-7348504-0-6

Divine Heart Connections
www.divineheartconnections.com

CONTENTS

Acknowledgments

I would like to thank all of my family members
and friends who have
helped me along my journey.

Preface

It is my wish to share with others my beliefs and spiritual awareness as I know it. Each day is a journey into the unknown. We learn in every moment from living and growing within our own spirituality. My goal is to provide a means of helping others to help themselves through this maze called life. The information contained herein is to be used as a guide for those interested in living a spiritual and/or healing path— a oneness with the universe and all that is. Let me say it is not my intent to demean or devalue anyone's religion or belief with the information contained herein. Please, take what you like and leave the rest; it is up to you to decide what works best for you and you alone. This is your journey, your path to enlightenment, and your spirituality, your healing; no one else's. Many blessings to all who read this book, and may you live a lifetime of continued hopes, dreams, happiness, unconditional love, and pure joy in all that is.

We are entering into a new world of spiritual awareness. People's mindsets and behavioral patterns are changing rapidly as we move forward to fifth-dimensional living and being in these changing times. We are in the process of leaving the monetarily-driven, industrialized society. People are learning that there is more to life than just money. We are learning that we have a spiritual side too. Spiritual reality exists if one can slow down to find it or it might even slam you up against the wall to say, "Listen, here I am." A new era is coming of learning to love ourselves, heal our bodies energetically, and live in the present moment. We are at the forefront of a changing society.

Change can be hard for some people; for instance, when Christianity was born, people had to hide in caves to practice their belief or else be chastised and ridiculed by society.

To handle ridicule for something you believe in isn't easy. This book is not meant to change your mind, but only to show you new opportunities or different ways of seeing spirituality, holistic (holy) healing practices, and talk about energy. What you are about to read in the next few paragraphs alone may get you thinking, "This woman is crazy." I have to admit, my initial response to the first book I ever read on chakras made me believe just that. I thought, "How can that be happening?" as I could not touch it or feel it. Or at least I thought I couldn't. It's a good thing I kept an open mind during my journey, because I have learned they are not so crazy after all. It is simply a different reality to the way I was raised.

Personal life experiences will be provided with illustrations about energy movement and the interesting things that happen. I have found that when telling stories of personal life experiences, people tend to relate and feel the experience and remember the information more readily. I do this out of love for you, the reader and human being, to help you grow.

Introduction

My Spiritual Journey

My spiritualness didn't start until I reached the age of fifty. To me, that's only a number. I have learned with living life that you are exactly where you always need to be regardless of age. My journey into the spirit world has been fascinating, to say the least. I've had many years of experiences learning how energy works, along with involving myself in ghost hunting activities and figuring out about the different types of energy out there; to what exactly ghosts are, and my personal favorite energies, divine energies. To avoid any confusion, I will refer to source, creator, and universe, as God throughout this book.

My family and I were not raised going to church. However, with that being said, my siblings and I had a great foundation with parents who stayed together, who helped support each other in times of crisis, provided for each other in times of need, and had fun with family outings together, just to name a few.

My great grandparents were farmers who helped to provide food for others. During the depression, since they lived on a farm, they didn't feel the impact so many other people felt because they provided food for themselves through their own hard work and gardening.

This is a lifestyle I believe we will be going back to in the future—organic gardening, and a much slower-paced society. When I was younger, I always used to have a garden. I loved putting my hands in the soil, feeling the coolness of the earth between my fingers when planting seeds and crops. Divine truly blessed my great grandparents because they provided food for the community through their hard work of farming.

My father was outgoing and would take us on adventures such as canoeing, hiking, and camping, that always took us back to the beauty of our planet we call Earth. Connecting with Mother Earth are experiences I believe everyone should have and appreciate. In my world of adventures, I never felt compelled or believed it was necessary to go to church in order to be a good person; to have good moral values and/or standards. My joy of God, my spiritualness is in gardening, camping, and being outdoors, in nature.

In other words, Mother Nature is my church. It's a place of meditation and quiet solitude. It's a place to experience the joy of living with the birds, animals, and simply the peacefulness in our surroundings. In nature, trees and plants give off what is called negative ions. Research studies indicate that negative ions help to reduce molds, mildew, and allergies in the air. Therefore, Mother Earth and nature are the places to be, in my opinion.

When I had my astrological birth chart read, I learned that I would become spiritual in my later years. I truly didn't know what that meant until I started my journey with becoming a Reiki Master/Teacher. My whole perspective on spirits and "the other side" totally changed after learning Usui Reiki (a Japanese spiritual healing modality that you can also call Universal Life Force Energy).

When you are attuned to Reiki, you are assigned spiritual healing guides to help you move and channel energy to create healing for your body and others. For those who are unaware of what a spiritual healing guide is, it's an energetic spirit not in a physical body, who is knowledgeable in moving energy. With continued practice of this healing modality, my intuition started opening, and my whole life changed before my eyes. As I worked on healing myself, my psychic abilities continued opening as the movement of negative energies left my body. As more and more energy channeled through my body via Reiki, my body was learning to send and/or channel energy to my clients. The palms of my hands used to ache when channeling the energy as the chakras in my hands began to open and channel more energy.

The more your body heals and releases old emotional traumas, the more energy you can move or channel through your body. This is why Reiki Level I is so important. You are working on yourself to heal. Reiki Level II is about healing others. When you work on yourself first, you will be in a much higher vibration to heal others.

As my practice increased using Reiki Level II, I started feeling energies change in the people I was treating, as well as seeing colors change in my third eye and/or sixth chakra. My psychic abilities were opening rapidly.

The more you heal yourself, the more energy flows through you, and your chakras rotate faster (more on chakras later). What happens is your body vibrates at higher levels and begins its own healing process. (We are indeed vibrational beings in a physical body).

Also, when working with Reiki clients, I soon learned that energy does not lie. If the person has something blocked in their auric body/energy field, you can feel the stuck energy in that area and that tells me what is going on with the client. I believe learning about energetic fields would be most beneficial in the courts of law, simply because energy doesn't lie.

On July 25, 2012, I experienced a spiritual awakening phenomenon. When I awoke that morning, I started to sit up in bed to start my day when an invisible force on my forehead (on my third eye) pushed me back in bed. Believe it or not, my first thought was I was being abducted by aliens. After that thought, a feeling of calmness overtook my mind and body. My eyes were closed, but I could see a spiral on the wall of my bedroom. The spiral formation of energy moved slowly from left to right. The outline of the spiral was black, but I could see web-like images between the lines that were moving with it. This experience lasted approximately five minutes and then everything went away. The force that had pinned me down on my third eye lifted. This experience was nothing short of a miracle. I can't explain who or what happened during those long five minutes, but I can tell you that my life has certainly changed for the better since my spiritual awakening.

Another memorable spiritual awakening was when I went to see a man from Croatia by the name of Braco. He stood at the front of the room, usually on a podium, where he would gaze into the eyes of everyone in the room. By this time in my journey, my body was able to feel a lot of energy, and what I was feeling was the most incredible energy, the highest in vibration I had ever felt. This experience was nothing short of amazing. Because of my participation at these events, I had no doubt a higher power (God) was responsible for what I was feeling. I went on to attend many more Braco functions where I saw many miracles of healings, kundalini awakenings, and increased spirituality for all in attendance.

Because of all of my experiences that are listed throughout this book, it is my belief that a congregation or a room full of people holds more energy and can provide more intent-making miracles happen than a single person. People can manifest and change lives by pulling together into groups, congregations, and communities and by tapping into Universal Life Force Energy to create peace and healing around the world! Be the positive force in your community to create and build ceremonies to promote health, healing, spirituality, and manifesting for the good of all people.

Mary Bannon

Chapter One
Energy – What Is It?

Universal Life Force Energy

It is my understanding and belief that you don't have to know any certain methodology of healing in order for Universal Life Force Energy that is all around us to work. All of us are natural healers. Every last one of us has the ability to heal ourselves and others. Just by placing your hand on someone's shoulder to let them know you care about them is healing to that person. It can lower their blood pressure, and it can calm them down almost immediately. When a child falls down and places their own hands on the cut or bruise, he/she is healing that wound. We just need to realize—believe–our body has its own innate ability to heal itself and when using Life Force Energy, it helps our body to heal itself that much quicker. My grandmother, who was not privy to this healing information, had arthritis in her fingers. She told me one day that when she placed her own hand over her fingers where the arthritis was, the pain went away. With this information, there are times when you are using Life Force Energy without even *knowing* you're using it. Even if I did tell her about

Life Force Energy, because of her belief system, she probably would doubt me, and that's okay.

First and foremost, I have learned that Life Force Energy is everywhere. You can find energy in humans, animals, objects, plants, and trees. Life Force Energy is not something that is for sale, but there is a way to capture or harness it and use it for healing yourself and others. There are many people who have created different forms or modalities of healing from Life Force Energy.

In the book, *Hands of Light* by Barbara Brennan, she indicates that Life Force Energy is those tiny little particles or "globules of orgone" that make squiggly patterns in the air. The next time you are enjoying nature at its purest, lie on a blanket outside. Watch the clouds drift by, and you might be able to see orgone for yourself. Look for those squiggly patterns while relaxing your eyes so you are focusing on absolutely nothing in particular. Looking with that soft gaze, you may see these tiny little particles of energy floating around. You've probably always wondered what those little squiggly things were. Also while you are lying on the blanket, look up at the trees. Defocus your eyes to the surrounding of the trees and perhaps you will see a white glow outlining the trees. This white glow is called their aura. This is the energy that trees infiltrate into the atmosphere.

To name a few of the various cultures that have captured this magical Life Force Energy are Japanese, (Reiki), Chinese (chi), pranayama (one of the five principles of yoga), Wicca or Celtic, and ancient Egyptian healing practices. The list could go on, but you get my point. The practice of Life Force Energy is known throughout the world. It's just a matter of what tools and intent we use to tap into it. Some people have become very creative with it, as in Kundalini Reiki, created by Shree Ole Gabrielson, wherein the intent has already been created and set for you and all you have to do is call in the procedure you want to do on a particular client for healing to happen.

Along my spiritual journey, I have learned many different methodologies of healing. I first became a Reiki master/teacher along with a few others (more on Reiki in Chapter 9). My teachers were wonderful. However, after class ended, there was no further training or instruction. I felt I needed to practice my newly found skill, therefore, I decided to start monthly Reiki shares. After some time, we met other Reiki masters in the community, and the Reiki share grew. If you are attuned to at least Reiki Level II, I highly recommend finding or creating your own Reiki share in your community to help you learn more about energy work as your vibration raises and grows.

Since I couldn't see energy, I was unsure if I was doing it correctly. I knew I was going through the motions I'd been taught, but I just wasn't sure if what I was doing was working or helping the person I was treating accurately. Learning the colors associated with each chakra helps the practitioner determine which chakras are out of balance, closed, or not receiving Life Force Energy. One day, I had the use of a Kirlian aura photography machine that takes pictures of a person's aura.

We had taken a picture of a client, and we could see for ourselves what colors their energy fields held. We took a before photo of the person that was to receive the Reiki treatment. It showed just a few blobs of the color blue, which is the color for communication, meaning the client's throat chakra was open and not blocked. She was able to speak and communicate so that information in the aura picture was definitely correct.

After a half hour session of Reiki, we took another picture, and the aura photo was an amazing and beautiful rainbow of colors. Comparable to the colors of all the chakra's being open and functioning properly. As you can imagine, I was filled with joy. It was simply amazing to me to learn this, as it gave me all the confidence I needed to continue along my path of spiritual healing. For me, seeing was believing. The person who took the aura picture asked the client to get into their heart space and rock back and forth from one foot to the other, as if she were rocking a baby to sleep. This turned her aura picture to a color of white with a speck of purple. This showed that she was totally connected to divine and spiritual beings and that her energy centers were totally balanced and aligned as they should be.

From that point forward, I was much more confident and comfortable knowing that what I was doing was absolutely helping the person receiving Reiki treatments. I felt so confident about working with energy and people that I made a conscious choice that day to continue along my spiritual and healing journey.

My next energy lesson was when I attended an Awakening Weekend to become a Deeksha Oneness Blessing Giver. This was a process created by the Oneness University in India for connecting each person more deeply to God energies. This process allowed me to open up to new beginnings and provided me with new divinely inspired energies and connections in my body. This program provides an opportunity to teach people to forgive themselves and others in order to be a clear channel for spiritual energies as our bodies hold onto emotions. The way to release these emotions is through the act of forgiveness with this program.

The Deeksha Oneness Blessing helps people to become awakened on their spiritual journey; it helps them to have and maintain loving relationships, helps to heal them, and allows new higher vibrating energies to flow through them. With each Reiki treatment or Oneness Blessing session, the recipient's energies and vibrations increase, and the healing continues for everyone, *including* the person channeling the energies.

My next step was learning to work with angelic beings as I was intrigued by this concept, and because I wanted to learn more, I went on to become a Master Instructor with a program called Integrated Energy Therapy ® (IET) created by Stevan J. Thayer.

I am grateful and thankful I learned this particular modality of healing. It is a wonderful way to feel the angels' energies being channeled through your body. It is nothing short of a miracle for the person who sends the energy, as well as the person who is receiving the new energies from the angels. I have had numerous successful healings and miracles with the IET process.

This modality works more with a person's emotions, as Stevan Thayer is also a Reiki master. He'd found it difficult to help a person release the emotions that were causing the pain with Reiki alone. He channeled Archangel Ariel's information, and the IET modality came into being.

There are several integration points on a person's body that release anger, resentment, victimization, and fear just to name a few. I've heard many people comment that this modality of healing is, "Reiki on steroids," meaning that it is very powerful; and it truly is.

My spirit guides then steered me toward working with crystals and stones that are so much fun to learn about! Crystals and stones have the ability to help move energy through the body as they too carry Life Force Energy. My spirit guides told me they could help me more if I used stones during healing sessions. Crystals are known to vibrate, transform, absorb, and transmit energy. Energy is everywhere, and crystals are the perfect conduit. With every healing session using crystals and stones over their chakras, people felt more relaxed, re-energized and full of energy.

During the same time period, I also learned how to work with crystals through the use of grids. Grids are a very powerful way to create and manifest your dreams, healing, or whatever you desire. You can create a grid for just about anything. To help you find the perfect job, spouse, or significant other, as well as getting the perfect night's sleep. The possibilities of manifesting your dreams are endless. (See more information about stones/

crystals in Chapter 8). Please check with your state regulations about the requirements for using crystals and stones with energy work.

As my spiritual journey continued, I decided to do a series called The Lightarian Ray Program. The Lightarian Institute for Global Human Transformation was established in 1997 by Jeannine Marie and Christopher Jelm. This program was so endearing to me as you first clear your energetic body with high level clearings via the ascended masters (AM) and Lord Maitreya. Then you move on to attunements with the ascended masters, archangels, seraphim angels, Aurora angels, and then the higher levels of Archurian, Sirian, and Pleiadian energies. These energies and the program are well worth the advancement in your energetic field and body by providing high level healing energies to yourself and your clients.

I was also intrigued with learning shamanism as it is considered the oldest religious practice for healing sickness (spiritual and physical), working with the spiritual world, crossing over the dead, energetic clearing of the land and houses, as well as cleansing and clearing the energy blocks in people most effectively through the use of quantum physics and changing and/or eliminating subconscious thoughts. I attended several workshops with Raymon Grace, a pendulum guru from Virginia, and with Catrin Jacksties from New Zealand.

Learning to meditate with the use of binary beats is also another way of connecting to your higher self for information. I have had the absolute pleasure of attending the Monroe Institute in Farber, Virginia, for their five-day programs which, for me, were extremely helpful in my spiritual journey. These programs help you go deeper into meditation by utilizing music made with binary beats. They are designed to help you grow along your spiritual journey because you are more than your physical body.

Psychic Development

It would be difficult to learn about energy and not learn about psychic development or how energy moves, and how a person who has psychic abilities can pick up on the energy moving. Please know that everyone is psychic. If you were lost in the woods somewhere, you would have to heighten your ability to listen for predators. The information you seek is all around you. All you must do is listen to your instincts and heighten your five senses. Psychic development is basically on the same principle. It's learning to develop the skills of seeing, hearing, knowing, and feeling with the knowledge from heightening these skills. There are some religious denominations who believe this is devil worshiping, but it is not. It is providing a means of getting closer to God, angels, ascended masters, spirit guides, and your loved ones on the other side. You do not need to go through the means of a traditional religious pastor to get closer to your understanding of God.

The following is a fun story. When I was developing my psychic abilities, I wanted to visit a friend who lived in a small town. I only knew the location of the small town itself. I asked this friend not to tell me where they lived in town because I wanted to use my intuition to find them. My strongest psychic ability is as an empath/clairsentient, which means I "feel" energy. As I drove along the small main street in town, I listened to what I was "feeling." Should I go straight? Should I turn right at this street? Should I turn left? I was listening to my gut instinct or feeling rather. As I drove through this small town, I listened to every gut feeling I was having. At one point I turned right. Then I was driving down a larger road. I asked myself, is this right? My gut instincts felt good about it. Then on the next road, I felt like I needed to turn right. I did and I drove slowly down a country road. This was a gravel road so there wasn't much traffic on it. As I slowly drove down the road, I didn't feel like I was getting much information from my guides. Then, as I looked around, I saw my friend's car parked in the driveway of a house only 500 feet away! I did it! I found my friend without having any address or directions. All the information I had was the location of a town. That was amazing! This is a very good way to help strengthen your clairsentient abilities. Your body knows everything and it's honest. I listened to the feelings my body was giving me and was taken to a physical location that I previously knew nothing about.

There are six main terms that are used to determine what our psychic abilities and/or gifts are. It is important to know every one of us has the capability of learning and honing our psychic ability skills. When we practice these abilities, they tend to get stronger because we are using them. And, you are heightening your skills by listening to your spirit guides as they are the ones providing you with the information.

The Six Clairs

CLAIRVOYANCE

This is the ability to see clearly through our third eye (6th chakra). This is the point just above your eyebrows and centered on your forehead. There are many people who are clairvoyant and can see spirits, as well as receive messages from their spirit guides, angels, or God through seeing signs and/or visions. You may even see a film happening, giving you a motion picture of what is about to happen or what has happened to you or the person you are working with. To strengthen this ability, you need to be more creative or imaginative with crafts, painting, or drawing to stimulate your third eye.

To strengthen my abilities, I had a friend help me. I asked them to think of a color and then I would hone in on their energy to receive the color they were thinking about. Or you can create cards with different colored construction paper, then draw some squares, circles, rectangles, triangles, stars, whatever you feel, on the colored paper. With your eyes closed, hold the paper up to your third eye and guess what color and image you have in front of you. You can also purchase some Zener cards. You will be amazed at the results you get. Although, if you don't get it correct, don't get frustrated, as this can lead to an energetic blockage. You want to be as relaxed as possible while doing these strengthening exercises to allow the energy to flow.

If you have clairvoyance, remember, you are working with your energetic spirit guides. Work with them daily. If you tell your spirit guides an apple means "teacher," then the next time you see an apple in your third eye, it means that a teacher is around you or coming into your future. You tell your spirit guides what objects mean and they will work with you.

CLAIRAUDIENCE

This is when you clearly hear the voices of spirits, either internally and/or externally. You may hear the voices in your head of someone who has died or crossed over as they are in the room with you. Sometimes the information is coming through to you in a thought form and it may be your own voice (in your head) that is talking to you. This one confused me for a while as I didn't realize it could be my own voice in my head; but it is actually a thought that spirits generate in your head for you to hear. However, there are times when you may be in a high EMF (electromagnetic field) where spirits can gather this energy and make sounds through it. For example, I was in a large electronics store to purchase something and all of a sudden, I heard my name being spoken out loud, and it wasn't a friend or neighbor. There was no one there. To hear your name being called out loud with no one there is pretty awesome. Definitely, a spirit was following me and wanted me to know they were there.

CLAIRSENTIENCE

Clairsentience and/or empath is the feeling of what is happening around you or feeling the pain from others. You can also feel the presence of spirits. You can feel what is going on with another person who is ill or has health issues. When you can feel the energy or you are sensitive to another person's energy, this is clairsentience. This can be dangerous for people who work in the medical industry such as a hospital or nursing home. They may pick up the energies from the people who are sick and carry this energy from pain and sickness out with them. Empaths need to learn how to protect themselves or cleanse their auric field on a daily basis. (See Chapter 2). My energetic body has risen so high in frequency that I actually get a headache from low-vibrating energy such as fear. This may be happening to you as well. People who are clairsentient don't like being in crowds or parties as their energy seems to get depleted.

CLAIRCOGNIZANT

This is a knowing of what is going to happen or knowing something that has already happened. Or you may just have the information, but you don't know where that information came from. This happens to me frequently when spirits drop by to see me, and I absorb their knowledge, or they provide the information to me. For example, when I purchased a Rune Set, I already knew how to read the runes without ever being taught by anyone or reading a book on the subject. There are also times when I work with a client that I can lay my hands on them and know what has happened to them. The information just happens to be in my brain already.

CLAIRGUSTANCE

I have not met many people with this particular "clair" so it may not be as prevalent as the other "clairs." This is the ability to *taste* a substance or the essence of a person's personality/character without placing anything in their mouth even though they taste it there. The person with this ability when "tasting" the person they just met, can determine what qualities this person may have and determine whether they like them or not through this sensitivity. This ability is a form of clairsentience.

CLAIRALIENCE

This is the ability to smell a fragrance that a person (spirit) may have worn when they were alive when the physical fragrance is not actually there. Some people who have this ability may also be able to gain knowledge about someone's character and/or personality just by one's smell. This also is a form of clairsentience.

All of the above abilities are because of energy flowing in and out of your chakras, as well as your 6th chakra (the third eye) and your spirit guides moving the energy by being a gatekeeper to your knowing. Your spirit guides, healing guides, angels, ascended masters, etc. all want to help by showing us and giving us information and ideas to propel us forward and help us move energy for healing ourselves and others. In Reiki, the spirit world assigns us healing energy guides to help us move this energy.

Ways to Open Up to Psychic Energy

- *Quit the use of caffeine*—this allows you to open up more where your body is not as tense and the ability to use your senses is much greater and clearer.

- *Eat a vegetarian diet*—this helps you to feel the energies more readily because heavy meats tend to slow down digestion.

- **Quit smoking**—this allows for the energies to flow better in and around your body.

- **Practice meditation**—this allows you to slow down and listen to messages from spirit, God, angels, spirit guides, or your higher self. When we want something so bad such as, to hear spirit, or to feel, we generally get tense because we want it to work. This stops the energy from flowing properly. When you are in that meditative state, make a conscious effort to feel if your body is tense, ask your body to relax as much as possible, take some deep breaths, focus on your breathing so much so that you feel you may go to sleep. When we are in our dream and alpha states, we are relaxed much more. A lot of times this is when spirit comes in to intervene because you are relaxed and in your "right" brain.

- **Laughter** and **dancing**—this helps the body to release being tense so that you have a better chance at listening and hearing spirits. When your body is no longer tense, the energy in and around you has better energy flow.

- **Crystals and stones**—they help with opening your psychic abilities. Here are a few suggestions: labradorite, fluorite, amethyst, emerald, white calcite, magnetites or lodestone, azurite, lapis lazuli, malachite, phenacite, iolite, and turquoise.

The different types of spirit energy that I have encountered are: God, archangels, angels, fairies, sprites, ghosts, gnomes, djinns, demons, succubus, and spirits, ones who have "crossed over" to heaven and ones who have not crossed. There are more; however, these are the ones I have personally experienced. A brief explanation of each is outlined below:

- **God** is our creator/source and he/she is the one who created Life Force Energy all around us. Both male and female energies exist within God.

- **Archangels** were created by God to help us, to answer our prayers. Archangels are very high in vibration and very pure. They will not interfere with your free will unless asked to do so, or you encounter a situation when it is not your time to leave this plane of existence.

- **Angels** were created by God to help God and the archangels. Angels are also of high vibrational stature and are very pure. However, be careful here as there are fallen angels. Please be specific when you call upon angels. Ask only for the highest vibrational angels for the highest good of all.

- **Fairies** have been known in folklore for many thousands of years. They are known to be human-like beings with or without wings. They have small energies, but they are powerful little beings. I know them to be in woodlands, gardens, around trees, and in the grass. I call on fairies to protect and help my garden and flowers grow bigger, stronger, and more abundant.

- **Sprites** are a smaller energy than fairies that help out whenever they can, when called upon.

- **Gnomes** are smaller energies who protect gateways, gardens, and other lands such as cemeteries or bridges.

- **Ghosts** are energetic beings who have lived here on earth. However, they have not crossed over to Heaven because they are attached to something or someone here on earth. Forms of attachment could be family, money, or personal items they are unable to let go of, or even religious beliefs, as they don't want to be judged by God.

- **Spirits** are energy beings who have crossed-over to Heaven (or different dimension). These are people who have actually lived here on earth and can come back to watch over you and help you in any way they can. Spirits can also come back to earth many times over, as in reincarnation.

- **Spirit guides** are the spirits (usually you have known them in previous lifetimes) who watch over you to protect you and guide you to your life purpose(s). There may be many spirit guides that are assigned to you helping you with your journey here on earth. Some guides come and go as you need them.

- **Demons** are negative entities with a consciousness that are evil and want to do harm to you. With everything, there is light and dark or yin and yang. They are able to move objects and can change your thoughts to make you think a certain way or even do things you don't really want to do. (More on negative energies in Chapter 2).

- **Succubus** is energy that is believed to be a female demon that has sexual intercourse with sleeping men.

- **Incubus** is energy that is believed to be a male demon that has sexual intercourse with sleeping women.

- **Djinns** are considered to be either good or an evil spirit by Arabic mythology. The Arabic meaning of djinn is "jinni" or demon. The djinns are able to shift their shapes easily to become humans, angels, or animals in order to deceive you. Therefore, be careful what you ask for when dealing with djinn.

- **Orbs of light** are energies of God, spirit, fairies, sprites, gnomes, spirit guides, angels, and also include dark energies, etc. Orbs of light carry with them a vibration and depending on that vibration will determine what color the orb will be.

I have experienced each of the energies listed above in one way or another through ghost hunting or through intuitive healing sessions with clients. My spirit guides have touched me to let me know they are there. I can feel the higher vibrational energies of the angels when they are present (because I am clairsentient). The fairies live in my garden, and I use their energies to help my flowers and vegetables grow. A few years ago, I had my picture taken while standing next to my six-foot tomato plant and caught the fairy orb coming out of the plant on camera.

My first experience with an orb of light was when I took my puppy outside during his first snowfall to play in the snow. He started running back and forth by the fence, and it looked as though he was chasing something. He had never acted like this before, so I got my camera and started snapping pictures. After I got him inside, I reviewed the pictures and was astonished to see a white orb. The picture captured him chasing after it. That was the first orb I had ever seen or captured on camera. Orbs are not things that the naked eye can see normally, unless you have that psychic ability, but they can be captured on photos or videos.

Man know thyself; then thou
shalt know the Universe and God.

– Pythagoras

Mary Bannon

Chapter Two

Protection, Negative Entities, and Energies

I believe that everyone should learn about what energy is. Energy comes in a variety of different vibrations. Low vibrational energies are considered lower dark negative energies. The higher vibrational energies are that of pure God-like angelic energies. Of course, there are mixes of both and in between. In my opinion, a person should know how to use protection from low vibrational dark energies and/or entities. There is a yin and yang to everything. Therefore, protection of yourself and others is imperative when working with Life Force Energy in clearing negativity from homes and working energetically with others. This information is not intended to scare you, but simply to allow you the information to know there are dark energies and entities out there. Learning how to protect yourself and others is crucial when working with energy. The difference between a dark energy and an entity is the negative entity has a consciousness and is evil in all of its behaviors. A dark energy is just energy created and left behind or imprinted and does not have a consciousness.

On the other hand, some people believe that if you are truly connected to white light and you are always working with God's highest vibrational white light around you, you will always be protected. These are good thoughts and intentions. However, when working with energy, you will come across someone you are clearing, and they may have a dark entity attached to them. If you go to extract this dark entity from this person, and you don't protect yourself, this entity may attach itself to you. In my mind, it is always a good idea to set an intent of protection prior to any healing or clearing work and ask that God, the angels, and your energy guides to surround you with God's white light and protect you. It only takes a minute, so why not take the extra precaution?

However, if you absolutely have no fear and you believe that nothing can harm you, then you do not have to set an intent for protection. A belief system is your thought forms that create a matrix of energies much like a spider web that is in your energetic field. You cannot have a matrix system that believes that something can harm you. It's like you have to believe that you are Superman and not have a belief that something can harm you. Also, you cannot have any fears or else the entity will find your weakest spots and plague you.

Demonic Manifestations

Dark entities are demonic in nature, in that they can direct negative thought forms into your energetic body, thereby controlling you. Once during a healing session with a client, this person had a dark entity that was intertwined and spiraled around their spinal column. This entity was demonic in nature as the energy was able to influence the thoughts of the person it held captive, plus it had an intelligence of its own. It knew we were going to try and extract it from the person. Through the use of intuition, it was deemed that the person had been held captive for many lifetimes, because the man this demon influenced in the beginning had "sold out" to it for power. This is called a Demonic Influence or Possession. With the help of divine angelic and ascended master energies pushing and pulling their energies through this person's entire body along with the use of a crystal crown chakra singing bowl, we were able to extract the demon. The dark entity, however, was broken up into smaller pieces due to the extraction.

Unbeknown to me, a small portion of the demonic force followed me home. I knew it was trying to get to me when I started experiencing bad thoughts that were not my own. My body was protected as I had asked for protection during the extraction. However, it had followed me home. Now I had to vanquish it from my home. If you find that you are having any feelings of dark thoughts or having thoughts of death and destruction that are not your own, please call upon Archangel Michael to surround you and demand that these energies leave you and your home at once. Anytime you have a demon or dark entity around, you must claim your space—demand it—and send it away. You cannot be wishy washy when you do this. You have to be a warrior to demand it to leave. Raising your vibrations in God Consciousness is also helpful when extracting dark entities. Another alternative is to contact a person experienced in this department to extract it for you. Although this gets tricky because if you believe it can come back, it will.

I also find that negative spirits/entities can attach to people. Many times, people in mental institutions can be plagued with dark and negative entities, spirits, djinns, and sprites that are antagonizing and/or disturbing them with their negative thoughts and feelings. This is the reason they don't feel good or they have continued problems in their life. I was doing a tarot card reading for a woman one time and the information coming through was not accurate. She indicated to me that another tarot reader was not accurate either. That's when the little bell in my head went off. I cleansed and cleared her energetic field. After that, the information came through perfectly. For the tarot card readers out there, if that happens to you, you will know what to do now.

Once I was camping with my parents and I was feeling a spirit moving through and around my body, including my private parts, while I was trying to sleep. More than likely it was an incubus energy as my thoughts started going out of control. They were not my thoughts as they were very negative, and that's not like me. My thoughts are normally very positive. Whatever this dark entity was, it was controlling my thoughts and turning my thoughts into negativity. To get rid of this entity, I started thinking, "*Go away! You are not welcome here.*" I was adamant and furious that this entity tried to take over all of my thoughts and control me. This is where you need to take complete control to get rid of it. After I felt it leave, I asked the angels to surround me and keep me protected as I slept. There were other people in the camper with me, and I didn't want to disturb them, I just thought these words in my head, and it worked.

Another client I helped over the years had a dark entity enter her body, and it changed her entire demeanor. Her whole attitude about life and everything around her was very negative, whereas, normally she is a very positive, loving person. Unfortunately, she had taken on the qualities of this negative entity that had attached to her. Why this entity was able to attach to her is because at the time, she was in a low, self-pitying state of mind and was vulnerable to dark entity attacks. This particular case took about an hour and a half to extract through the use of shamanism and quantum physics.

Things to look for if you believe a negative entity has attached itself to you:

- a sudden loss of energy
- the feeling that someone is watching you
- acting totally out of character
- a loss of self confidence
- a sudden illness that cannot be explained
- negative obsessive thoughts
- irrational fear
- thoughts that are not yours

This is just a small list, but it is important information.

One time I was ghost hunting at a local old firehouse, and I felt a sudden surge and draining of energy in my body. Number one, I did not protect myself which was a costly mistake. Number two, a ghost had just entered my body and took my energy. At least, the entity was not negative, but this is just my point that the entities and spirits are out there, and you could fall victim to them if you do not protect yourself.

An example of a **prayer for protection** when doing energy work might be: "*I call upon the archangels to surround me, protect me, guide me, and direct me, for the highest healing (or good) for (name of person you are healing or sending good vibes to).*" I have found that this prayer works very well every time.

A very strong protection for other purposes such as ghost hunting or places where you know dark entities may inhabit is: "*I call upon the highest vibrational Godhead energy to surround me in a column of God's white light. This light protects me. This is my light. I claim it. No one else may have it. This light surrounds and protects me at all times. This light cannot be taken by anyone or anything. And so it is.*" This prayer is very effective and may even raise your body temperature as the light is very pure and high in vibration.

If you believe you have a demonic negative entity or spirit attached or inside of you, it would be best to consult with a local professional energy healer and have them extract it for you. This is not something that you should deal with on your own as it could create more havoc.

Negative Energies
(not of a demonic nature)

Negative energies can be anywhere in the world. Negative entities, spirits, and dark energies can be picked up almost anywhere there are negative people, emotions, or where thoughts exist. They are at restaurants, grocery stores, banks, gas stations, liquor stores, etc. When you visit the local market, there may be negative energies in the building because the person running or working in the store has negative energy and is criticizing and being negative all of the time. This creates an atmosphere of negative energies and they may attach themselves to you. Because the items in the store sit in a place that holds this negative energy, unbeknown to you, you are purchasing and carrying negative energy home with you.

People can create their own negative energies just by their thoughts alone. I performed a healing session for a teacher who worked in an elementary school. When I placed my hands on her, I could feel something was attached to her abdomen. It wasn't malevolent as it didn't feel like it had a consciousness to it or that it wanted to do any harm. In actuality, this person had created this thing in her own mind because of her fear of being alone in school while she was grading papers. As you can see, your mind is very powerful.

This type of energy is called a Larvae and/or Psychic Parasite as it is something that is created with the mind of the individual. To extract it, I had another energy worker at her feet while I was at her head. We created an energetic wave with all of our healing guides, angels, and God wherein we pulled and pushed energy through her body until this energy she'd created flipped off of her. I felt my healing guide's hand at play during this extraction—like the warrior he is—come through to help us. The client was very happy to be rid of the energy because her energy changed to a much lighter, freer feeling.

The Kabbala teaches us that demons can be our own negative energies, demons feed off our fears, and fear is the lowest negative emotion you can create. I believe the demon called on here is our shadow self. We all have negative energies within us, such as negative thought forms, and it is our job to learn what they are and cleanse and clear them to the best of our ability.

Demons are generally negative entities who have a consciousness, are evil or malevolent. They do feed off fear because fear is the lowest vibration. Negative energies are just low vibrations of energy. For example, if you and your partner have an argument, you are leaving behind negative energies with all the things you are saying and creating with your thoughts. Negative thoughts create lower vibration which brings us to the topic of depression.

Typically, the cause of the depression is the person's own negative thinking, unless the depression is drug induced or a chemical imbalance in their brain. There are many depressed people who have created their own low energies and low self-esteem, along with negative energies or Energy Vampires that live on their body. The depressed person now becomes a host for the parasite. I have worked with many depressed people and find they suppress their emotions, as well. It's their own thoughts, possibly through childhood programming, that are creating the depression along with the suppressed emotions. By changing a person's thought patterns through positive affirmations (see Chapter 5) you will create a better, more positive and higher vibrating human being. Energy work such as Reiki or the modality of your choosing will also help depression because you are moving the negative energies, parasites, out of the body and the aura. However, unless you change the person's negative thoughts and thought patterns, the negative energies will be back, and the depression as well. Personally, I utilize the two-pointing modality (quantum physics) for releasing depression quickly and efficiently by changing the programming of self-limiting beliefs.

Negative energies are drawn to people who are always criticizing, or bursting with anger, rage, bitterness, and resentment. All types of fears can also draw negative energies to us. You are also at risk for drawing negative energies to you if you abuse drugs or alcohol. Smoking cigarettes has a tendency to leave holes in your auric field and, therefore, you are vulnerable to negative energies penetrating your energy field.

Cleansing yourself of negative energies

Cleansing and clearing negative energies from your body will help in raising your vibrations. It's a good practice to cleanse and clear yourself daily. Listed below are many actions you can take to cleanse and clear yourself.

An ancient custom used by Native Americans, proven over many centuries, is burning white sage to clear negative energies from your aura. You can purchase white sage at a metaphysical shop in your area. When burning the sage, be sure to have something to catch any loose burning ashes that may fall from the stalk. Wave the burning sage in and around your aura and body about 6-8 inches from you, making sure not to burn yourself.

Another way to remove negative energies from your aura is to take a white selenite wand and with your intent of removing any and all negative energies, move it through your auric field to clear yourself. This is my personal favorite way of removing negative energies. I also keep a white selenite tower at my front door entry to absorb any negative energies that attempt to enter my home. You can use this same technique with hematite, black obsidian (known as the protector) or black tourmaline, which are also great stones for helping to remove negative energies.

You can also clear your aura during your morning or evening shower by envisioning the colors of all the chakras and moving the energy in and out and through your body with your thoughts and visions.

Used for centuries, the Tibetan monks in Nepal have created a wonderful incense that has all the essential oils necessary to dissipate negative energies. Using this incense helps to lighten a room from negative energies because of the essential oil properties in the incense. Your local metaphysical store may carry this item called Nag Champa.

Using sound vibrations through crystal or brass singing bowls, Koshi, or Tingsha bells also dispels negative energies due to their vibrational nature. Another personal favorite of cleansing and clearing away negative energies and creating higher vibrations is through prayer. I pray over my food, my drink, my clothes, my home, and my vehicle. Not only do I pray, I also utilize positive intentions to bring in higher vibrations of love, peace, happiness, and just plain good vibes. This helps keep your body, home, and vehicle in good higher vibrations (tip top shape) at all times.

Something else you can do, if you are a visual person, is to imagine a white bubble surrounding yourself to protect you from any harm or negative energies. You can use a pink bubble for protection to put love into the equation since pink represents unconditional love.

For example, I like to place (through imagination) a pink bubble every time I jump in the car to go somewhere. Its usefulness is good for trips, long or short. Visualizing a pink bubble is good for protection from negative people who criticize all the time or even from arguments. Perhaps you don't like a person at work, and you want to protect yourself from their energy and negativity. By all means, use that pink bubble to protect yourself.

Please read as this is very important.

If you have an energy practice such as Reiki, please be sure to wash your hands after each session, as well as cleanse your area and/or massage table. Negative energy may stay with you and your area after client sessions. For example, during a Reiki share, a person placed their hands on top of my head to channel energy to me. Because she had not cleansed herself off after a client prior to me, all of the negative energies she pulled from the prior client were now on me. The energies were so stagnant and sticky, I no longer had a connection to divine energies. Eek!

Cleansing your home of negative energies

Homes that have been lived in before carry with them the energy of the people who resided there previously. The energies of the prolonged pain of those individuals can remain even though that person no longer resides there.

At a house cleansing I performed, all of the negative dark energies of the woman who had lived there previously were still there, attached to the house. No judgment here, but she was an alcoholic, and her husband tended to her needs. He, himself, was feeble and could not walk or care for the home any longer and so they moved (all of this information was received psychically). When I first got to the house, I felt nausea. There was just an overwhelming sense of dread. The basement was the worst place where negative energies had gathered because the woman sat in the finished basement daily playing solitaire and was simply an unhappy soul. I called in the angels' powerful energies to lighten the entire house with their higher vibrational energies. We also created an angel vortex where the entire family could pass through to receive the healing power of the angels on a daily basis. This was placed at the back door entrance that the family passed through every day.

You can basically use the same methods of cleansing and clearing your body for your home. You can use white sage and smudge the home to remove negative energies. When using white sage, you will walk in the front door and start at the very left corner of the home, light the sage (being careful not to allow any embers fall), and work your way around to each and every room from left to right. When you get back to the front door, you push out all unwanted and negative energies and/or entities and seal the entrance with the thought that these energies are no longer welcome in the home. If the home has a basement, you would start in the room to the left of the stairs, work your way around to the other side, and swish the energies up and out of the staircase. Then, you start again at the main level and move your way around with the burning sage from left to right through every room and out the front door. The entire time while walking through the house, you will want to open your heart space with love and state, "I bless this home with love and light". This process works best when your heart is open, you call in the archangel of Choice, and channel this angelic love throughout the house/building.

After you have cleansed your home from negative energies, you can place black tourmaline, black obsidian, or white selenite to absorb and/or deflect any negative energies away from the house, objects in the house, and you. Placing a piece of hematite on either side of both front and back doors can deflect negative energy away from your home.

Negative energy and/or entities can also attach themselves to objects. Therefore, if an object has spent its life in a home that only had negative energies in it, the object would carry this negative energy with it wherever it goes. Someone who is sensitive to energies and is around the object, may get negative energy attached to them from the object. This is called psychometry when you have the psychic ability to touch or hold an object and receive information or history about it. I'm sure you can ask any antique dealer for stories, and they would be able to tell you about negative energies being attached to objects! To rid your object of these negative energies, again, use the same methods as before. You can also call in the angels and ask for their loving guidance and assistance and set your intent that the object be removed and cleared of any negative energies.

When I use crystals and/or stones, I cleanse them by placing them on top of my white selenite wand. You can do the same with objects just by placing black tourmaline, black obsidian or white selenite on top of objects or under the object depending on how large the object is. From this point forward, your energies will be the only energies your house and objects will absorb, so keep your energies light and fun!!

Psychic Attacks

Psychic attacks are made or created by people who are knowledgeable in voodoo, spells, curses, and witchcraft. This involves summoning up dark energies, entities, and spirits, and moving them to people to attach to and possibly sending these dark energies/entities to their homes as well. This is done to hurt the person involved. This is another reason to ask the divine angels and energies to always surround you and protect you. If you have an open heart, and your auric energy field is strong and happy with Life Force Energy, then it is harder for these types of energies to penetrate. However, if your energy field is not strong, you may need to ask for assistance from your local pastor or contact an experienced energy worker for help in getting rid of the negative energy/entity for you.

Unfortunately, not all people are kind, compassionate, or considerate. There are some people who are dark and pretend to work in the light. I was working a psychic fair, and there was a woman also working the fair several booths away who was jealous of me. She threw all kinds of spells and curses at my heart to try and bring me down. She did not succeed as my heart captured this negative energy, hardened it, and it fell to the ground before it got to me. This is an example that when your heart is pure and full of love, you are divinely protected.

Another way to deter a person who is sending you bad vibes is to place (in your third eye) a mirror around you to deflect the energies being sent. This is not my favorite because it sends the negative energy back to them. Negative energies feeding negative energies does not teach the person anything until they are ready to learn that this type of behavior creates karma for themselves. Personally, I like to send all negative energies, curses, hexes, and spells, to the sun to be destroyed. That way, no one receives the bad energy. I also ask that the archangels wrap that person in unconditional love. When you fight back with love, the other person has a tendency to stop fighting as they are filled with love. Love is a higher vibration than hate, anger, fear, and jealousy.

In another example, I was again a participant at a psychic fair. This man who considered himself to be a healer was across the aisle. A psychic medium next to me didn't seem to like him much. He saw our glances toward him, and he apparently jumped to conclusions, thinking we were talking about him. He sent a psychic attack (bad thoughts of wanting to hurt us) over to us. After feeling these negative and rotten energies, I knew something was wrong. I immediately blocked what he was sending over and then asked for Archangel Michael's protection, as well as asked for God's white light to surround us to ward off his vicious attack.

This behavior is not in the code of ethics for a healer. A true spiritual healer only wants to help others attain a wonderful healthy life. Please do not tolerate unacceptable behavior from anyone. You should always have healthy boundaries. It is unfortunate that some people who portray themselves as healers can act and treat others in that manner (lessons they need to learn). It would be in your best interest to stay away from these types of people. Never send negative energy out to others, only send love and healing regardless, but by all means, protect your energy at all times.

Some people believe in hurting others because they felt hurt by them. This only adds to the negative energies around us. Fighting back is a natural instinct for survival. However, what has just happened? Negative energy is being fought with negative energy. However, if you can, for just a moment, put yourself in the other person's shoes and think that if this person is learning a lesson they need to learn, what happens then? What do you get? *More negative energy!* This goes back to negative energy attracts negative energy and positive energy attracts positive energy— The Universal Law of Attraction.

You can create a positive outcome when you are not putting negative energy into the situation. Keep your vibrational energy raised and intact by not responding negatively to other people's situations or life lessons.

I realize at times that not to react to bad behavior can be difficult to do. What I would like for you to do for just a moment is to consider the other person involved and the consequences surrounding the issue or situation. Consider the person who is objecting and fighting. Perhaps their survival skills are the only thing they know and they do not know love. Love heals all things, including hurts from the past, present, and future. Be the light and the example, hold your light for them to see and learn.

When you are around spiritual people, the energy in the room, place, or house is lighter. For example, I know a person who went to India and met Sri Bhagavan, who teaches Deeksha or Oneness Blessings. While there, she purchased a ribbon that had been placed around Sri Bhagavan's neck for one entire day. When she brought it back to the United States, she allowed me to touch this ribbon and feel its energies and vibrations. It was amazing how you could still feel this person's higher vibrational energies in the ribbon. You could actually feel the ribbon vibrate with Sri Bhagavan's enlightenment with God source energies. Placing this ribbon in a room could ward off many negative energies.

There have been times that I have experienced negative energies while driving. If a road has been placed on an old battleground or where people have been killed, hurt, and maimed, the energy of that battle is still there. Once I was taking an exit ramp while in Florida and felt a tight band around my head. (There was another empath in the car who felt it too! Confirmation is always helpful.) Apparently, a person had an automobile accident there, and the head was involved with killing that soul. This is an energy imprint. (More on energy imprints in Chapter 8.)

It's important to help the earth evolve and transform negative energies from places such as old forts and battlegrounds, Native American or otherwise. These are energy imprints left upon Mother Earth from horrific battles that occurred there. There are also ghost soldiers and warriors who are still out there wandering around because they were killed so quickly they don't realize they are dead. I make it my goal to help these lost souls to cross over to the other side whenever I can. (There is more on crossing ghosts over in Chapter 11.)

Because of free will, it is
with our cooperation and assistance
that the angels, spirits, and divine can
help us with manifesting
our truest self.

Mary Bannon

Mary Bannon

CHAPTER THREE

Connecting to Healing Guides, Angels, Spirit Guides, and Ascended Masters

Because I have been working with the angels for more than a decade, I have learned they can change your DNA in a matter of minutes. What you hold onto energy-wise can be wiped away, and you can have a clean slate, so to speak, by learning new ways to think and to forgive those around you who have hurt you. The angels and other higher realm beings are here to help us upon our asking. Since we have free will, the "asking" is the key.

When performing healing work on yourself or others, and when you tap into Life Force Energy (white light), it is to your advantage that you call upon God, healing guides, archangels, deities, and/or ascended masters for the highest good for all concerned, including yourself. In the last chapter, you learned that you need to protect yourself from the negative energies and now you are calling in the higher vibrating realms to help you tap into Life Force Energy.

Because we live a life of free will, it is up to you to call in your choice of the highest vibrating spirit and/or entity to help manifest and create healing for you or someone else, as they will not interfere with free will. The only exception to this rule is if you are in an accident, and it is not your time to leave this plane of existence. The angels may intervene in that case.

Regarding all archangels, seraphim angels, angels, sprites, fairies, spirit guides, and loved ones on the other side, all you need to do is ask for their assistance, and they will be there for you. It is best that you be as specific as you can when calling in these energies. For example, you can just call in the angels and archangels, and their energies will be there. The angels do not have free will. The angels are here for us by God's Divine Law, and they are to act to the needs of God. The angels are to be the bridge between God and all of its manifestations throughout all dimensions, not just this planet or galaxy for that matter. Unfortunately, there are angels who have fallen. If you want the best, you may want to call upon the highest vibrating angels to help you.

All of the above beings of light have the ability to separate their energies so that they can be at many different places or locations at once, including other galaxies. Therefore, do not feel as though you cannot call upon them because you feel they are needed elsewhere. Their powers are so big that we as humans cannot ascertain or even understand their power and strength. Just because I address them as he or she, they are able to balance the masculine and feminine perfectly. They come to you with the energy they know you need at that time.

Plus, you don't have to stop with just these entities. You can call in the power of animals such as lions, elephants, birds, and so on. If you are familiar with the energy of certain animals, for example, by calling on the elephant's powers you will be calling in strength, wisdom, gentleness, and confidence to name just a few characteristics of the elephant. You might want to use their strength and characteristics when going on a job interview.

I have listed a few entities that you can call upon to help you in your times of need and healing for yourself, as well as for others. Although each angel or master has its own vibration, just because they have a title about them as to their purpose or job, that doesn't mean you can't call upon that angel or entity for help in a different area of your life, if you feel intuitively led. At the end of the list, I give examples of how you would communicate or ask for the angel or master to help you.

ARCHANGEL ARIEL

Overseer of the World. Angel of Destiny. She serves to oversee the protection and healing of animals, fairies, nature spirits, nature elementals, minerals, and plants. Call upon her for environmental causes such as cleaning up environmental disasters. She brings us opportunities for abundance. She helps guide us to our true purpose in life. Color is pale pink.

ARCHANGEL CHAMUEL

Angel of Love. He embodies the power of love to help build strong relationships, improve communication between the people involved and repair any misunderstandings. He can help strengthen your connection with others by releasing old grievances and insecurities and expanding your heart chakra. Color is pink.

ARCHANGEL GABRIEL

Angel of Communication and Angelic Joy. He is known as a great communicator for the divine. He can help you create a feeling of pure joy and harmony within yourself. He can also help you access your "knowing" or intuition. If you are writing a book, call on Gabriel! Color is white.

ARCHANGEL HANIEL

Angel of Bravery & Determination. She can help you create a more joy-filled life by teaching you not to look outside of yourself for joy. Rather, joy is created by being in the moment and letting go of all fears that stop us from being in pure joy. She can help with our sense of reason and logic. Color is orange.

ARCHANGEL JOPHIEL

Angel of Wisdom and Divine Beauty. She can help when you need clarity or insight or are faced with difficult choices or decisions in life. She also teaches that the power of light is within yourself. Helps you to create a sense of joy and happiness. Color is yellow.

ARCHANGEL METATRON

Angel of Universal Wisdom. He is the guardian of the Akashic records. He can help you find the knowledge that you seek. He teaches people how to balance their energy and use their spiritual power for good. Color is flashes of brilliant white light.

ARCHANGEL MICHAEL

Angel of Protection and Power. He helps us build and expand our gifts for telepathy, etheric communications or channeling, as well as astral traveling. Considered a Leader. Color is blue.

ARCHANGEL RAPHAEL

Angel of Healing and Courage. He will provide us the courage needed in our goals for global and human transformation. He is known as the Divine Healer and assists us in the process of healing. Color is emerald green.

ARCHANGEL RAZIEL

Keeper of God's Secrets and the Angel of Mysteries. He is known to help heal your spirit of hurtful memories or painful trauma by removing blockages or deep memories stored in your body. He also helps you to release any vows from past life experiences and release any phobias or fears you may have. He can also help with loyalty issues. Color is rainbow.

ARCHANGEL SANDALPHON

Prayer Gatherer or Angel of Art. She teaches truth and the power of prayer. She can assist you with connecting to your inner spiritual world. Color is turquoise.

ARCHANGEL URIEL

God is My Light or Angel of Beauty. He helps us to expand our appreciation for beauty that surrounds us and stimulates us in our own expression of beauty through our creations— for example, writing, or channeling. Color is ruby.

ARCHANGEL ZADKIEL

Angel of Mercy, Purity and Compassion. Zadkiel means, "the righteousness of God." Zadkiel helps us to feel compassion towards ourselves and others. He helps us see the divine light within us and others. He helps with forgiveness. Color is purple.

SAINT GERMAIN

Keeper of the Violet Flame. Call upon him for the gift of prophecy and freedom or to deepen your connection to your divinity. Use his assistance in prayer to invite all nations to put down their weapons and attain peace and enlightenment for all. Color is deep purple or violet.

ASCENDED MASTER JESUS

He is the most famous story of ascension. He will help you to know that you are God, know that you can perform miracles, and help you to release all beliefs that you are separate from God. He can help you with forgiveness, love, and the misdeeds of judgment.

MOTHER MARY

She embraces divine femininity, infertility and birth, but most of all unconditional love. Call on her to heal your relationships, create abundance and to follow your bliss. She knows that only love is real and that everything else is just an illusion.

LORD MAITREYA

He is called "the compassionate one". He is the Master of all Masters. He will help you to connect with your life's purpose or to use love and cooperation to create anything.

ASCENDED MASTER KUTHUMI

He is the master of light, love, wisdom, and understanding. Call on him to clear your subconscious mind of all unsettled issues, release any limiting beliefs, and attain mastery.

ASCENDED MASTER BUDDHA

Buddha is a Sanskrit word meaning "awakened." He will help you to quiet your mind, experience love/compassion for all, and see the truth in all things.

ASCENDED MASTER EL MORYA

He helps us to manifest with one's life purpose and align that with God's will. He is a powerful and beautiful connection of absolute pure love.

ASCENDED MASTER SANAT KUMARA

He is called the "holder of all wisdom and learning." He will help you to cleanse your home and life from all negative influences. Invoke his presence to light the sacred fire within your heart.

LADY NADA

She is the protector of children, helps to empower our truth within ourselves, and brings justice to life's challenging events.

She also reminds us that what we resist becomes stronger and whatever we embrace and love dissolves into nothingness.

WHITE BUFFALO WOMAN

She is from the Lakota/Sioux people. Call on her as she can activate your sacred purpose, fill you with a sense of peace and joy, as well as, see the divine nature in everything.

ENOCH

Call on him when you need to successfully complete writing projects, bring justice to any given situation, and deepen your spiritual knowledge and power of the Zodiac.

Learning to invoke the presence of angels and the Master's energies is easy. All you have to do is ask. Let's practice. The first thing we do is call upon our protection.

> *Dear Mother/Father God, please surround me and protect me from all negative energies and entities. Cover me in your white light of love and divine energies to keep me well protected. This energy is mine and no one else may have it. This white light is impenetrable to all dark energies.*
>
> *Thank you. Amen.*

You can call in your angel, ascended master, or saint, for example:

> *I call upon Archangel Raphael to surround me in my hour of need. Please guide me and heal me*

*and provide me with the highest level of
healing. Help me to release any negative
energies that no longer serve my
purpose or desire.
Please and thank you. Amen.*

You can ask God to provide you with the healing and allow God to assign the task to the angel, ascended master, or saint of his choice for the situation. Either way, you can ask, set your intent, or pray, and if it is of the highest good for all concerned, it shall be done.

If you are an energy worker and you want to set up a fast system of calling in the energies you want to work with quickly, then you would open your heart space, call upon your protection, set the intent with each entity you want to call in, then ask each entity that *(for example only)* when you touch your right index finger to your thumb, you are calling in each one of the energies and spirits to help you with your manifesting and/or healing. Now each time you touch your thumb and index fingers together, you have just called in your entourage of helpers. Now granted, it doesn't always have to be your thumb and index finger for this; you can come up with other creative ways as well, such as touching your hand to your ear. It doesn't matter what it is as long as you set the intent for that to happen. Just ask, and it shall be done.

Personally, I have received attunements through the Lightarian Ray Program to the ascended masters wherein their energy(ies) are there for me whenever they are needed in helping others to be healed. All I have to do is ask for assistance, and their energies are there and easily channeled for the highest good of all concerned, including me.

Sometimes it's difficult to know if calling in the angels, God, and/or ascended masters or praying over something really works. Here's a personal story regarding that. One of my family members was very ill and was placed on a ventilator in the hospital. We had no idea if they would survive. I, as well as many others of my family, called upon God and the angels to help in our hour of need. When I got to the hospital, I knew that our prayers had been answered as I could feel the presence of God and the angels' energies surrounding this person. My family member is alive and well today. Intent setting and prayers truly do work if it's meant to be.

*O*nce you let go of negative people,
positive people appear.

Unknown

Mary Bannon

Chapter Four

Intent Setting, Prayer, Forgiveness, and Gratefulness

Intent Setting and Prayer

One morning I woke up and heard the words (via clairaudience) "It's all about intent." I pondered this for a very long time and finally came to the conclusion that if you intend for something to happen, you think about it (thoughts are energy), and then it is created and/or manifested. The natural law of attraction dictates this. Your mind is a very powerful tool, more powerful than we can ever imagine. If you think about it, a prayer is a form of intent. When you are praying, you are thinking about good intentions and therefore creating them.

Some people create and/or manifest with spells, which is nothing more than setting your intentions and therefore creating and manifesting what you want. There is nothing bad about spells unless the intent or thought is bad or not for the highest good for all concerned. I know everyone thinks that if you are a witch, you must be bad. *Wrong.* There are bad people, and there are good people, and there are good intentions, and there are bad intentions. If you think about the outcome as being helpful to the person and/or to the good of the universe, then how can a spell be bad?

Let's take a look into the differences in practicing with energy. Each practice is based on the motives with which someone uses them. Here is a list of those practices:

BLACK ARTS PRACTICE

The black arts have only one thing in common: the person using black arts wants to be in POWER. In these cases, the black arts practitioner basically sells their soul to the devil in order to get what they want. This includes human sacrifices, ritualistic rape, and other evil practices.

DARK ARTS PRACTICE

This type of practice is used against people because the practitioner believes they have been wronged and they are trying to make it right for themselves. It's a sense of righteousness to justify their action—an eye for an eye. A person's ego is generally involved here.

NEUTRAL PRACTICE

This type of practice is not considered light or dark (good or evil) as their intention is "as long as it harms none, do as you will." For example, creating an intention (or spell) to attract money could be, "By the power of the moon and positivity, bring now to me wealth and prosperity. Bring forth to me, with harm to none, so be it." This type of practitioner goes with the flow.

LIGHTER ARTS PRACTICE

This type of practice is mainly used to help and assist others. This will include various forms of healings, blessings, cleansings, and protection based on a love or service-oriented practice. The practitioner knows the dangers of dark forces and uses their knowledge to protect themselves and others at all costs. This type of practitioner has a strong code of ethics and honor that prevents them from giving into their shadow self.

WHITE ARTS PRACTICE

This type of practice goes beyond the ego and becomes pure in thought and deeds. You would need to be a pure channeler of divine energies. Basically, this type of practitioner frees themself from the energetic matrix and becomes one with all. The dangers of the white arts is when you open yourself to all energies, you let in the dark energies too. This openness can attract astral parasites and negative entities. The thought process of this type of practitioner is that if you are only working in the light, and you are utilizing the dark energies/entities, the light will transform the dark into light. You definitely need to be cleansed and cleared of all your fears and thoughts that you cannot be hurt because the dark will prey on all of your misgivings and weaknesses.

Monks use Life Force Energy when performing intent setting, prayers, and chants. When you repeat something over and over again you are creating a plethora of energy of thought and intention. With their purity of soul, opened heart chakra, as a large congregation of pure energy, monks can create and manifest intentions like a power plant. So why isn't our world free of chaos and murderers? Bottom line is, you cannot heal or fix someone who is not ready to be healed. That person who is on hard times or bad luck must learn their own lessons. This is why we are here on this planet Earth—to learn lessons that help us to ascend to higher states of consciousness, to experience this beautiful world, and to love. Getting back to our highest state of consciousness is *love*. In other words, everyone has free will.

If we set our intent on winning the lottery, why haven't we won yet? Cynthia Stafford is someone who has used the principles of the Law of Attraction and has won the lottery many times. She has shown us by focusing all of your energy/intentions on winning the lottery, dreams can come true by winning. If you use the Law of Attraction for money-making purposes and you don't win the lottery, chances are the universe has different plans for you. Perhaps you have a different contract with the universe for being here, and it doesn't include being a millionaire because then you wouldn't learn the lesson you came here to learn in this lifetime.

Send energy or set an intent/prayer for your garden and flowers to grow, to be healthy, and to be abundant. I use Sacred Geometry symbols in my garden and ask the fairies to watch over it to help the garden grow. My flowers and garden are generally very healthy and abundant.

Here is an example of intention setting and prayer. One morning, I was getting ready to go to a Oneness Blessing event.

After I showered, I sprayed rose water over my heart space and asked that Mother Mary walk with me that day to send healing and blessings to all the people attending the event. This was my intent/prayer. During the event, a woman came up to me and said, "Did you know that Mother Mary walks with you, and she is sending everyone here blessings and sprinkling rose petals over all of us?" I was elated to know that my prayer and intent had been heard and actualized. Now that is what I call confirmation. Keep a listening ear or ask your spirit guides to bring forth confirmation of your intentions and prayers. They can be very powerful.

Thoughts are energy. Intentions are focused thoughts. Now let's put worry into the picture. Is worry a thought? Is worry a focused intention? When you worry are you drawing that focused thought to you? The answer is a resounding yes. Worry is nothing but a negative thought. It's time to turn those thoughts into positive thoughts and intentions to bring what you really want into your life.

It is with my greatest pleasure to share this next portion of the intent-making process with you. When I participated in the Al-Anon group, I heard stories from people all over America who stated when they got down on their hands and knees and prayed to God they were at their last rope, their last hope of surviving this terrible disease called alcoholism; they submitted themselves to God, and healing began and miracles happened. Basically, they set their intent that they no longer want to live this way and are no longer in control of themselves.

The person starts feeling better about themselves and they start on a healing road to recovery. With God's grace, the person has set an intent; they have submitted to God; they have asked for forgiveness (Step #8); they have let go of total control and see what happens? Miracles abound in this universe.

It is only my opinion that the 12-Step program is one of the best programs out there for repairing and helping people who suffer from addictions. It doesn't even have to stop at addictions. The program also helps people who have suffered from abusive relationships or people who have been raped, molested, sexually abused, etc. Basically, the 12-Step program helps people who have been emotionally distraught and injured through the curse of other people, which brings us to the topic of forgiveness.

Forgiveness

Forgiving anyone and everyone who has hurt you is an important step everyone should learn. This is a topic most people try to avoid and ignore. Some people believe forgiveness is for the other person. Instead, forgiveness helps the person who is doing the forgiving with the ability to release from the heart all of their pain. That is a gift in itself. The first thing to learn right now is: forgiveness is not for the other person. It is for *you*. When you forgive others of their wrongs, you are opening *yourself* up to the ability to love. It is freeing your energy in your body to a higher potential and raises your vibration and frequency.

It is also important for Lightworkers to go through the same process of forgiving as this allows more energy to be channeled through the healer to their clients. Your heart chakra will become more open and the energy will flow more freely and easily. You will be a clear channel for Life Force Energy or spiritual healing to flow to its intended recipient.

Please note that you are not accepting that person's behavior. You are allowing yourself to let go of *your* emotional ties to that incident or situation with the person who wronged you.

The act of forgiveness opens your heart to the possibility of loving everyone and all things, including yourself. When you forgive someone for their wrongs, remember they are only human. They, too, are learning from their mistakes. No one is perfect. Most importantly, don't forget to forgive yourself for the mistakes you have made in your life along the way.

Let's try an exercise to help us open ourselves up to the loving act of forgiveness. This process was learned from a shaman, an energy worker of light.

Perhaps you can record the following on a voice recorder. That way you will be free to just enjoy the releasing process and not worry about reading the dialogue.

First, you will want to play some light music to help you relax. Sit in the lotus position or in a chair with your feet flat on the floor. Use the breathing technique of counting to five, breathing in to the count of five, and out to the count of five. Do this several times.

Now envision yourself surrounded in white light. Ask your angels and spirit guides to surround you and protect you. Begin to focus and feel your heart space. Feel your heart beating in your chest. Slowly and carefully open your heart to forgiveness and start forgiving everyone that comes to mind. Remember, you are not forgiving or forgetting what they've done or accepting their behavior. You are allowing yourself to let go of the emotional ties. State to yourself and the angels that you want to let go and cut all ties to the situation. You are safe. You are enjoying this time by yourself and letting go of these emotional ties to people who have wronged you. Take the time necessary to fully feel these emotions letting go of you and freely leaving your body. Allow for your emotions to release. Feel free to cry if that's what you need to do. It's okay. You are safe. Pause.

Now it's time to forgive yourself. Think about the mistakes you have made, people you have hurt along the way in this crazy world we call life. Let the emotions go. They are no longer wanted or needed in your life. You can start from this day forward with being the person you want and know you truly are. You are a child of God. A child of Divine Light and you are love. Feel the freedom that this release brings to you. Pause.

Once you are finished with this process, take some more deep breaths. Ask God and the angels to surround you with white light and completely fill you up with white divine light. You should make this time for you and you alone. Allow this to be a quiet time for you to reflect upon yourself. It is a time to love yourself and a time for healing yourself within. Pause.

Be sure to take all the time that you need for this exercise. I would recommend that you do this once a week for a month, so your body doesn't get overwhelmed.

Sometimes, emotions go deeper into the body wherein help may be needed by an energy worker. My spirit guides directed me towards a female massage therapist who also happened to be a shaman. While I was waiting for my appointment time, my spirit guides started showing me in my third eye all of my past boyfriends who had mistreated me throughout the years. When I told the woman what I saw, she knew that my body still held onto the emotional ties. Once she removed the emotion that plagued my body, it was easier for me to use the process of forgiveness. Unfortunately, it took a shaman to help me remove my emotions because they went really deep into my muscles and central nervous system.

The forgiveness process is also important to the Oneness University when you become a Oneness Blessing Giver. You go through an intensive day just letting go of the pain others have caused, remembering who we are and forgiving each family member and/or friends or spouse(s). Again, we have another culture that believes in going within and the art of healing ourselves.

Gratefulness

This chapter would not be complete unless I spoke about gratefulness. Being grateful opens us up to new possibilities.

I learned how to be grateful for what you have when I was married to my ex-husband. This is not to give him a bad name, but to give you information as to what I went through in my journey of loving a man who refused to help himself. He is an alcoholic. This unfortunate circumstance gave me the opportunity to join a fantastic group of people called Al Anon. This group literally saved my life. The 12-Step program is a program that is not to be doubted. It works if you use it and set your intent for a happy, healthy, and wise life. This program allowed me to find myself and have the ability to learn who I am. By working the 4th step, "to take a personal and moral inventory of yourself," I was able to learn who I am. Now remember this is a journey and not something that is attainable overnight. You must put effort into this process because you are learning all kinds of things about yourself. This process made me stronger and soon I had my self-esteem back. I'm not saying just work the 4th step, I am saying that this is the step that worked miracles for me. Working the entire program, I learned that being grateful for everything in my life, the happy, the sad, the indifferent, even my ex-husband, and learning from those mistakes is what makes me who I am. However, I am not the trauma, and neither are you. Forgiving the trauma and all that happened is another journey which is all a part of this particular program.

Soon after my husband and I divorced, I met another man and I fell in love. I was very happy, but I didn't know or understand it when this man decided to commit suicide. I was devastated. I thought my life was over. I also lost my job during this time period as well. It was the lowest of lows in my life, and I had hit rock bottom. Little did I know at the time, it was going to be a new beginning for me. After his suicide, he came back in spirit and basically haunted me. He wanted me to know that life on the other side does exist.

When he was alive, we had talks about whether or not there was life after death many times. This is when I learned spirits really do exist, truly an eye opener for me.

To let me know he was around me, one night I was watching TV using the remote control to flip through the channels. I came across the movie, *There's Something About Mary*. He used to tease me about that movie all the time. At the same time the movie came on, my stereo turned on all by itself. My stereo had never done this before, and it never did it again. At the time, I just chalked it up to there being something wrong with my stereo, although something in the back of my mind kept tugging at me thinking it was him, letting me know he was still around.

In just a few days, another incident happened at about 4:00 in the morning. I was lying in bed and had just awakened. I was laying there thinking to myself how devastating my life had become and started crying softly to myself about all of the sorrow in my life and in my heart since his death and losing my job. I felt like I had reached my breaking point. My hands were lying on top of my chest on top of my heart. Suddenly, my chest started vibrating (that's never happened before or since) and I could feel something or someone squeezing my hand! The vibration lowered in my chest and the squeezing of my hand ceased. Again, the vibration got higher, and I could feel someone squeezing my hand, but no one was there. Each time the vibration got higher my hand was squeezed. This happened three times. I was elated to say the least. After that experience, I absolutely knew he was with me, and I knew that there is life after death.

From that moment forward, I started talking to God, I told Him how I was very grateful for everything I had and all that I have been given in this lifetime, no matter what. I knew every event that happened to me was a part of my journey and/or experience and a part of my life lessons. It was another spiritual awakening if you will.

I believe that being grateful for even the smallest things in my life that I had, and by thinking with positive affirmations every day helped me get my life back on track. I was thankful for my bed that I was able to sleep in, the food in my stomach, and the roof over my head because basically, that's all I had. After a few weeks of being grateful, my life started getting better and returning to some type of normalcy, if one can only imagine. I believe that being grateful in everything helps one to open their heart space to allow love to flow in.

I believe there was a reason I lost my job. I soon found another that gave me lots of new opportunities, and I was able to start my own business with a very dear friend and co-worker. Learning to be grateful in all that you do or have helps create and manifest a peaceful, loving life.

*T*he happiest people don't have
the best of everything,
they just make the best of everything

Unknown

Mary Bannon

CHAPTER FIVE

Focus, Positive Affirmations, Pranic Breathing, and Purity of the Soul

Focus

Focus on your intent and then get your ego out of the way. Yes, it is that simple for some people; for others, not so much. Sometimes it helps to place your focus on a symbol such as Metatron's Cube or a Cross (Chapter 6 talks more about symbols) because it helps you focus your intent on what it is you want to manifest.

Focus is what is needed for angels, God, universe, spirits, and healing guides to know exactly what you are working on or wanting to create. Therefore, focusing and stating exactly what your intent is may be helpful to your results of manifesting. Once you have stated your intent, you need to allow your ego to get out of the way. You're not the one who is creating the healing or manifestation. You are the channel or conduit for it to happen.

One day, I was standing in front of my sliding glass door, allowing the sun to shine on me for its warmth. With my eyes closed, I could see the sun's light on my eye lids. As I let go of control of my thoughts (meditative or alpha state of mind) my third eye or the color behind my eyelids changed colors. I saw the brightest of reds. Knowing that red is a sign of being grounded I thought I would change my thoughts and move up my chakras. My intent was to change and move my thoughts to my sacral chakra for which the color is orange. Done. The light behind my eyelids turned to orange because my intent changed to my second chakra. I did this for every chakra. When I got to my fifth chakra, the color is normally indigo, but the color was a bright, golden-white light. Bright, golden-white light at the third eye is the symbol for having a consciousness in the 5th dimension according to Joshua David Stone's book, *The Complete Ascension Manual.*

It was interesting how easy it was to focus on the energy of each chakra that brought about the visual change of color in my third eye. Focus and intention helps to create and manifest everything in your life. With this information, you can focus on the life you want without doubt and achieve it. If you have any doubts whatsoever, such as a thought form, "I am not good enough," that is an energy blockage that needs to be cleared.

Positive Affirmations

Understanding the natural law of attraction teaches us that thoughts are energy. What we think, we create. If you are always thinking negatively, you are bringing negative things to you. If you think positive, hmmm, not so hard to answer that one, now is it?

You are the co-creator of your life. You are what you think. Think positive thoughts every minute of every day. The flow of energy follows your intention. You can manifest the things you want in your life by creating the energy around it. There is a right and wrong way of attracting what you want or don't want in your life also.

The right way is to open your heart and bridge those *heart-felt* feelings and emotions to your brain so that every thought is felt and created out of love. By doing this, you are creating helpful, loving intentions and providing them to the world and everyone in it. By bridging your heart to your brain/thoughts, you can manifest everything you want to bring to you and the world.

In my life experience, I was lucky enough to have a business partner teach me how to be a more positive person. This woman is the most positive person I know. She came into my life when I needed it the most. After all, I did come from a divorced, alcoholic home with my ex-husband, and he was the most negative person in the world. Not that all alcoholics are negative, mind you. Just that mine was. She taught me how to be positive. With having an alcoholic ex-husband, I saw first-hand how a negative person draws negativity to them and then I saw how my business partner's positive mindset was able to manifest and bring new clients, to her and me, and new higher-paying jobs in our business which was incredibly *positive*. For me, this was another eye opener.

By using positive affirmations on a daily basis, one can bring to oneself the life they want and deserve to live. With the energy you put into being a positive person and always thinking and saying positive things, you will create and have the life you want in no time. Be patient with yourself. It takes time to let go of having a negative attitude, but it can be accomplished. You may want to find books on positive affirmations and use them daily. If you are around people who are negative, try weeding the negative people out of your life. Only be and communicate with positive people who love you and care about you.

If it is someone you can't say goodbye to, such as a mother or close relative, don't accept undesirable behavior. You can, however, be there for them, lend them a listening ear, love them with all of your might, accept them for who they are, and then go home. Your positive attitude by being around them and loving them may rub off on them after time. However, please remember to never accept undesirable behavior from anyone at any time.

Every day you wake up, you have a choice to be happy or to be sad. You create your life whether it is hectic, yelling, hitting, screaming; or you can be calm, serene, peaceful, joyful, and loving. Which do you prefer? The choice is yours every day of your life. With the use of powerful affirmations to change your thinking, you have the power to make these changes and these choices.

I have learned in my journey that you can turn your life around with positive affirmations. Being an Al Anon participant for many years, I learned that being positive brings positive situations into your life; after a while, you no longer want to be around the negative situations. In Al-Anon, we used positive affirmations to help change our thoughts and feelings about our life. Then the happiness and love that you are feeling becomes a part of your life.

This also applies to your health as I have learned from Louise Hay. She has taught us many things about positive affirmations. I highly recommend her book, *You Can Heal Your Life,* written in the 1980s, but it still stands true today. This book has a list of the symptoms and/or illnesses that needs to be healed or changed along with the positive affirmation you can recite every day to change your body and mindset into a more positive and healthier you.

As a cancer survivor, Louise beat the disease with her positive thoughts and proper nutritional diet. We are what we eat, and we are what we think. She was living proof of that. Unfortunately, since the writing of this book, Louise has passed away at the age of 91. However, her legacy of positive affirmations and learning to love oneself still continues to this day.

How this is applied to our thinking is that our thought is *energy.* Our body consists of many cells and our positive thoughts and affirmations change the structure of these cells. Negative thoughts change the molecules in our body, and when we have positive thoughts, our molecules change and repair themselves into a healthier version of ourselves.

When working with clients, I have found this to be true. Your thoughts have everything to do with disease and how you respond to situations.

Mastering the mind is how you will heal your body today and in the future.

Another book I highly suggest reading is *The Hidden Messages in Water*, written by Masaru Emoto of Japan. This man performed extensive research on water that helps us to understand how water changes through thought patterns and prayer. Mr. Emoto discovered through his extensive research that water is deeply connected to our individual and collective consciousness. He showed us that water, in a frozen crystal form, shows us its true nature.

For example, Mr. Emoto discovered how water crystals change with different thought patterns. If you have the thought, "I hate you, you make me sick," this has a substantial effect on the water. The crystals turned into a mucky looking substance with these negative thoughts. His research has shown that when thinking through prayer and positive thoughts, the crystals repair themselves and are happy and vibrant.

If you think about it, your body is made up of 70-80% water within your blood, skin, muscles, etc., so what is happening when you think negatively? The chemistry and DNA in your body changes for the worse. Negative thinking creates negative energy in your body. When you are down on yourself and you say, "I hate the color of my hair," or "I hate my fat body," or "I don't like the way I look," what are you doing to yourself? You are creating a negative you who needs love and attention. Wouldn't you rather have love than hate? So, please stop putting yourself down. Create a new you with positive thoughts and affirmations. I am beautiful, I am loving, I am worthy. These statements *will* create a positive you along with a healthier more vibrant you.

We all learn valuable life lessons at our own pace, but there is one basic truth we all learn early. Positive, compassionate words comfort and heal a person. Negative words and insults hurt everyone. Until recently, we knew this only because we could feel it. Now we can actually see it. Thanks to the experimental work of Dr. Masaru Emoto, we can look to water, and its frozen crystals, to confirm the healing power of beautiful music, positive thinking, uplifting speech, and prayer.

Pranic Breathing

Pranic Breathing is a simple breathing technique that helps us to quickly access the deepest levels of our mind. Pranic breathing is also used to focus our breathing on something specific such as healing ourselves or others. The use of pranic breathing is important in opening yourself up to be a clear channel for energy to travel through your body. It also allows you to focus on your breathing and ultimately Life Force Energy will get stronger as you breathe.

The techniques will clear and heal your own body. Once your body is healed, you are a clear channel for sending healing energies to others. I practice pranic breathing at every healing session and have had amazing results.

An example of pranic breathing in a healing situation for others: I was attending a healing circle at a Spiritual Church. I put my left hand up into the air like an antenna for spirit. I then cupped my right hand outwards from my heart. I was taking in deep breaths at slow counts of five, and then releasing the breath slowly. As I was deeply breathing, energies grew heavier and stronger. The prolonged breathing created an energy vortex so to speak, and there was an energy shift in the person being healed. Everyone in the circle could feel the heightened energy and shift. Realizing what spirit had done through the use of pranic breathing was an exciting moment for me—definitely something to try and practice.

Purity of the Soul

There really is no one way to do healing work. However, I have learned you cannot heal someone who doesn't want to be healed or who is not ready to be healed. A person needs to heal in their own time and space. It is not up to us when they are ready. That person may not have learned the lesson they came here on earth to learn. All we can do, as healers, is send the healing—prayers, thought, intent—up into the universe (for their highest and best good) and ask it be given when the person is ready to be healed. I teach this because of my experience in the Al Anon group I attended. You can only control yourself. You cannot control anyone else. You can help teach someone if they want to learn. As the old saying goes, "You can lead a horse to water, but you can't make him drink."

It is not up to us to change a person who is content always being negative and is happy with where they are in life. It's up to them to hit rock bottom, and then perhaps they will ask for help. When they do ask for help, it is assured that God, their spirit guides, and angels will provide for them what they need to get better. Then the angels can tap into the healing that you sent to that person. Everything we think, say or do is recorded. This is called the Akashic records. Archangel Metatron is the angel in charge of the Akashic records.

Here's a story about sending healing into the ethers for when a person is ready for healing to happen. I went to a pizza place in a little town in Indiana. On this one occasion, there was a group of people in the corner of the dining room who looked like they had a little too much to drink. One was a young girl who could barely walk from whatever drug or alcohol she had been partaking of. My heart went out to her. I immediately connected my heart with the angels and sent healing from across the room. My intentions were for her highest and best good for when she is ready to live a life of happiness and joy. I don't know when that will be. However, when she is ready, you can bet the angels will be there, sending her the healing sent to her that day. The intent has already been created and placed into the universe, and the universe will comply with the healing when she is ready, no questions asked. Don't worry if you don't have permission; send the healing to the highest and best good for when the person is ready to receive love and healing energies.

The first and foremost quality of being a master of energy is the power of love. For the utmost quality of love to happen to the master, one must love oneself first. If you are not able to look at yourself in the mirror and say, "I love you," then you probably need to learn some steps to get there.

One of the best ways I used on my learning path to loving myself was Step 4 of the 12-Step program. Take a complete and moral inventory of yourself. Write down the pros and cons of who you are today. Be honest and patient with yourself as this is a process—a journey if you will—and change does not happen overnight. Review your list and start consciously changing some of the things on your cons list for change to happen, one at a time so it's not so overwhelming. This process may take years, or it may take months or even days, depending on you and how hard you work on yourself for change to happen.

My favorite prayer for this process is, *God, Grant me the serenity to accept the things I cannot change, the courage to change the things I can, and the wisdom to know the difference.* When I was able to love all of the things about who I was, it gave me confidence to stand in my power because I knew myself through and through. No one can knock you down because you have a handle on everything about yourself. Once you have conquered the gift of loving yourself, it will be time for you to move on to the next part which is compassion.

Compassion

The ability to release judgment and not criticize the person who is lost, confused, and needs help with healing their body, mind, and spirit is compassion. It is a feeling of empathy for another human being who is hurting. As you know, it is not up to us to judge others. When we don't judge others for their mistakes, lifestyle, etc., it opens the heart for us to be able to detach from circumstances and situations. As judgment is a lower vibration, keep your vibrations high and think twice about judging others. Plus, when you don't judge others, this allows for energy to flow freer between the master of energy and the person being healed. That you may want to control the outcome is one of the reasons why a person may not be able to heal a family member. You cannot control it. You can only send the intent with love and ask for assistance for the highest good of the person receiving the healing.

Working energetically through the heart chakra when providing healing is paramount for miracles to occur. Everything is energy, and we, as energetic beings, are made up of vibrational energy. Scientists at Heartmath, with research of over two decades, have found that our heart generates the largest electromagnetic field (EMF) in our body. The results of their research have proven the heart has 60% greater EMF than the brain. This is the reason why our hearts need to be clear of past hurts so when we are the conduits for divine energy, Life Force Energy can flow freer from us to our client. The heart is the key, for without love, we are nothing.

Detachment from the outcome of healing is the best tool to have because it is not up to us to force our will onto others. The universe may have another plan for the person you are trying to heal. I learned a great phrase while in AlAnon, *Let Go and Let God*. Release the outcome because we are not the ones in control, God is. Learn to set aside your ego. Play and have fun, because the more you play and have fun, the more you begin to let go of your ego. Thus, more healing and miracles will happen. Good luck.

The three C's of life—Choices,
Chances and Changes.
You must first make a Choice to
take a Chance or your life
will never Change.

- Unknown

Mary Bannon

CHAPTER SIX

The Power of Symbols and Sacred Geometry

Sacred geometry has been used for many thousands of years by builders from all over the world in the construction of churches, mosques, monuments, temples, megaliths, altars, and other structures. Plus, architects have been using sacred geometry in the design of the buildings for long periods of time. Their drawings have created geometrical lines within the structure of buildings, including geometrical shapes on their own. Sacred geometry consists of straight lines, circles, triangles, vertical and horizontal lines, along with many other forms.

Using symbols and sacred geometry in your everyday life is extremely powerful and will help to bring in Life Force Energy and make it stronger for you. Egyptians, Lemurians, Atlanteans, Essenes, Tibetans, Japanese, Chinese, Indians, East Indians, and many other cultures around the world have used these symbols along with creating many other symbols to depict certain intents for healing and increasing/raising levels of consciousness and vibrations.

It is important to state here that when you believe (belief of your intent) that the symbol is used for these purposes, then that is what it is for. You could state your intent for something else if you so wanted, but you would have to use it for that purpose until such time you state your intent that it should be used for something else and clear the energy matrix from the old intention. However, if you continue to use the symbol for the same purpose repeatedly, it shall make the symbol stronger for you. Remember, it's all about intent here and what is right for you. Before using a symbol, you could sit with it in hand and ask what its best purpose could be used for.

SPIRAL

 The spiral is a female energy as it is curvy in its shape. I see this symbol more often in the décor of restaurants and hospitals. The spiral has been placed on many ancient buildings, tombs, and hieroglyphs around the world. This symbol can be seen in snails, as well as in nature. This symbol represents energy vortexes and energetic worm holes in the cosmos.

THE PEACE SIGN

 I can imagine that every country knows the meaning of the peace sign. This is a very powerful symbol as it carries both male and female energies together by using the straight lines as well as curvy lines. You can use this symbol to create the inten-

tion of peace around the world. Create a crystal grid and place the peace symbol on top of a map of the world in the grid and use it as your focal point for healing and peace.

FOUR-POINTED STAR

One morning I woke up and saw a shining star in my third eye. It had four points to it, sort of like a cross, but filled in like the diagram to the left. It reminded me of the star they used to depict the wise men who followed the star to the babe Jesus in Bethlehem. I was overwhelmed with feelings of calmness and purity. I believe it was a sign from heaven that divine energies support me. After researching the symbolism of this particular star, Native Americans believed the meaning to be a sign of courage and purity of spirit.

METATRON'S CUBE

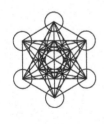

This symbol is extremely powerful when used. Metatron's cube represents every shape in the universe in one small package along with both male and female energies. Also used for personal transformation; it can change human DNA in an instant. This symbol is able to raise your vibrations to gain access to the Akashic records. When I meditated on this symbol, it said its true name is Babel, Akkadian language (bail) which means, *Gate of the*

Gods. The symbol's purpose may be to balance your energies for ascension to higher dimensions.

CROSS

The cross is a symbol of Christianity and one of the most widely recognized symbols in the world today. According to Christian belief, Jesus died on a cross made of cedar, wherein he died for our sins. This symbol is extremely powerful when used as you draw in Jesus' strength and love.

THE ANKH

An Egyptian hieroglyphic character, it is thought to be the symbol of life. You will see this symbol engraved on tombs and in art with Egyptian Gods holding it by the loop. There are many theories to its uses and meanings. Through time, one theory is that the ankh symbolizes life and immortality.

The symbol on the left represents the Egyptians' generator to increase a person's vibration. Use of this symbol may be to place the symbol on top of you, perhaps closest to your heart to increase you or your client's vibration. Notice the straight lines and circle representing both yin/yang energy. The symbol on the right is the Egyptians' symbol to transfer vibration into the body. Use of this symbol may be to transfer an object's vibration into you or your client.

THE FLOWER OF LIFE

 The Flower of Life is 19 complete circles and 36 partial circles, enclosed by a large circle. Leonardo di Vinci studied this in mathematical terms and found that all the platonic solids can be found within it. Metatron's Cube can also be found within the Flower of Life. This symbol is a creation pattern for everything in existence. You can find this symbol represented in the dimensions of Stonehenge. It is also represented in the architecture designs on temples located in China, Israel, Japan, Spain, Italy, and Turkey. The Temple of Osiris located at Abydos, Egypt, may be the oldest symbol, as the symbol may have been burned into the rock of the Temple and not carved.

THE SEPHIROTH OR THE TREE OF LIFE

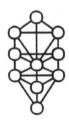 From within the Flower of Life comes the Tree of Life. This is a recognized concept within the Kabbalah and within Jewish religion. This symbol is called the "cosmology of the Kabbalah" because it was used to understand

how God created the world. The Kabbalah describes different levels through which the structure of the sephiroth (or Tree of Life) is functional in channeling divine creative life force.

THE PENTAGRAM

The five pointed star had various meanings in ancient times, i.e., five senses, five wounds of Christ; or in religion, the symbol for Wicca, Serer, or Druze. Another meaning is the top point is spirit, right point is water, bottom right point is fire, bottom left point is earth, and left point is air. It allows all five elements to come into the energy of whatever you place this symbol on. Inside the Pentagram is a special number, The Golden Ratio, which equals 1.618. However, the occult or darker forces have created an inverted pentagram with the two points projecting upwards, which to occult leaders means it overturns the proper order of things.

THE SEPTAGRAM

The seven-pointed star is known particularly for planetary magic as it points the powers of the seven planets of astrology in its balance. You can possibly view each point in the star as belonging to a planet.

THE TRIANGLE

This symbol has very masculine energy wherein it has three straight lines connecting into points and points direct energy. Anytime you have the number three, you can relate it to divine energies of the trinity.

THE STAR TETRAHEDRON

Fire energy is two tetrahedrons merged together. The star tetrahedron is also known as the Merkaba—the Mer meaning Light, ka meaning spirit, and ba meaning body. The most common arrangement of the water molecule is in the geometric shape of the Tetrahedron and water supports life. According to ancient times, one of the functions of the merkaba is to act as the vehicle to take the spirit and the body into the next world. The merkaba is considered the chariot of ascension.

THE STAR OF DAVID

The hexagram is the most popular and universally recognized symbol of the Jewish people. However, this symbol has only been associated with Jewish religion for only 200 years. Prior to that, this symbol was recognized with magic or the insignia of individual families. Either way, I recognize the power of this symbol as being "as above so below," as the two triangles point "above" and "below." Wearing this symbol on your person would help to balance your energies to divine and to Mother Earth respectively.

THE SHRI YANTRA

Nine different shaped triangles forms 43 triangles in all. It is a symbol of Hindu philosophy of the vedas. The triangles represent the cosmos and non-duality. The four upward pointing triangles represent the masculine energies, while the five downward triangles represent the female. When I meditated on this symbol, I felt it represents multi-dimensions of the cosmos. I learned to use this symbol for retrieving lost souls or body parts during traumatic experiences, as well as to clear past life karma. In mental health issues, it can be used to bring back scattered energies or bilocate to bring back energies from the past.

The Platonic Solids

HEXAHEDRON
Earth Energy

OCTAHEDRON
Air Energy

DODECAHEDRON
Ether Energy –
prana

ICOSAHEDRON
Water Energy

TETRAHEDRON
Fire Energy

The ancient Greeks have studied these five different shapes extensively throughout time. Plato associated these shapes with the elements listed beside the shape. An interesting note is that the tetrahedron (fire), hexahedron (earth), and octahedron (air), can all be found naturally in crystal structures.

The Golden Ratio (phi)

The Golden Ratio is sometimes called the golden number, divine proportion, and golden proportion. Phi is God in a mathematical approach. Its measure is always equal. God created the universe in a geometric plan. Is there a divine number embedded in our numbering system?

In Summary

You can use any of the symbols listed here in your manifestation or healing practice. You can place the symbols under a massage table or have pictures of symbols on the walls. You may want to meditate on each symbol to find which one draws your attention and feels good to you for your use.

Work with these different shapes in your manifesting or grid work. Get to know and learn their power through meditation or use. A six-foot Tetrahedron when created from copper and large enough to sit in is a very powerful conduit of energy. A one-foot copper Tetrahedron will keep fruit within its bounds from spoiling as quickly.

You can also wear these symbols on your body or wear them as a pendant to help make your Life Force Energy stronger to you. My personal favorite is the Star of David symbol. I wear the masculine side outwards for protection as it strengthens my energy field around me.

When providing healing to yourself or others, you can use any of the symbols listed here on a blanket or sheet. Then place the blanket/sheet on yourself, healing table, or person being healed, and that symbol will imprint its energy into the person or object you have placed it on.

An amazing and powerful technique I have seen recently is using symbols with a Henna prayer tattooed on your hand chakra or if you are a cancer patient and your hair is gone, place the tattoo on top of the head on the crown chakra to receive the prayer and energy of that symbol into the body for healing. The henna plant is a symbol for transformation, and what a great way to heal with the use of a symbolic prayer tattooed on your body. The ink from henna is not tattooed on with a needle. The ink is safe for pregnant ladies and the ink lasts 10 to 14 days and will fade after that. Please note that when people receive real permanent ink tattoos on the body, it could cause the energy to be redirected inappropriately. Just be careful with what symbol is being used and where it's located, especially when the tattoo is in a permanent state.

In recent decades, crop circles have been created by forces unknown to man across the world. Yes, some are hoaxes and created by man; however, there are crop circles that are so intricate there is no way man could have created them. These are the ones that are created by unknown forces. These geometric patterns are also creating energies and raising the vibrations of the earth. Hoax or no hoax, the vibrations of the earth are being raised for reasons unknown to man. My theory is that they are to help humankind in raising our vibrations as we leap into the Golden Age of ascension.

We don't have to stop here as there are many symbols in the world today. There is energy in plants and animals, and therefore by wearing the symbol of an animal or plant, you are creating their energy in your auric field around your body. You take on the qualities and character of that particular plant or animal. For thousands of years, the universe has been our teacher and guide through all of these various symbols and the energy they create.

*L*earn silence. With the quiet serenity of a meditative mind, listen, absorb, transcribe, and transform.

- Pythagoras

Chapter Seven

Power of the Moon, Elements, Yin/Yang, and Mother Earth's Energies

Power of the Moon

Other influences of energy you can use in your life and/or healing work is to learn and work with different moon phases. You may have heard that the emergency rooms in hospitals are generally always full when there is a full moon or that a woman will go into labor during a full moon. The full moon creates a plethora of energy that can be tapped into when setting intents, prayers, and/or spells. The *Farmer's Almanac* is written with the power of the moon and tides for when is the best time to plant your crops for the best outcome using and tapping into the energies of the moon and tides. In the days before TV, cell phones, and gaming, people were connected to the land and used the energy of the LAND and MOON. Gravitational and electromagnetic forces of the sun and moon create the rising and falling of our sea levels, called tides. However, it is the moon's gravitational pull that is the stronger since the moon is much closer than the sun.

Shamans and Native Americans, along with many Wiccan rituals set their intent or conduct prayers/intent/spells during full moon cycles and tides. You too, can learn to tap into it, use it, and manifest healing or manifest your dreams with it.

NEW MOON

The new moon has always been associated with new beginnings. This is a time to set your intentions for increasing business, new contracts, or even new relationships with the beginning of the new moon. Also, you may find this time is ideal for new adventures, planting or sowing the seeds for new ideas, or perhaps looking for new opportunities and growth for yourself or others. The new moon is the perfect time for change. Doing a food fast is beneficial during this phase of the moon as this is the time when the body has the greatest capacity to rid itself of toxins.

WAXING CRESCENT MOON

The waxing moon grows in size as it progresses from the new moon to the full moon. Since the moon is growing, it is the perfect time for *your* growth, for example, relationships, monetary, or for learning. This is the perfect time to attract new things in your life. Use this time also to create intents for healing your body and to store energy and regenerate yourself. The crescent moon could also be utilized for organizing possible resources for seeing your vision come to fruition.

FULL MOON

The full moon is the most powerful phase of all. This is a time when people have heightened psychic awareness and enlightenment. This is a time of family and/or friends coming together. Any intent, prayer or spell is the most powerful during this time of the moon phase. This phase of the moon also brings about manifestation or progress towards your goals.

WANING MOON

The waning moon decreases its size as it progresses from the full moon to the new moon. Use the waning phase to physically, emotionally, or energetically clear and discard any unwanted people, business or behaviors in your life. This is a time of reflection, letting go, and a time of completing those tasks or projects. End the things that no longer work in your life during this phase of the moon. This is the perfect time to rest and regenerate.

Elements

By raising our spiritual consciousness, we raise our ability to be aware of the energies that surround us, either visible or invisible. The four subtle energies; Earth, Water, Fire, and Air are the building blocks of creation. Our astrology charts are based on these energies and are comprised of our personality traits and characteristics. Many of the great philosophers, mystics, alchemists, and spiritual teachers around the world have found these energies similar to their own categories of expressing the elements of these energies. It is also found that these energies make up characteristics and/or behaviors of people, companies, games, etc., everywhere. The following is a short introduction to these elemental energies and what their predominant attributes are.

FIRE ELEMENT

The fire element characteristic consists of yang or masculine traits. Fire energy is associated with the qualities of strength, courage, enthusiasm, power, creativity, and persistence.

EARTH ELEMENT

The earth element characteristic consists of both yin and yang (the feminine and masculine together). Earth energy is associated with the qualities of consistency, responsibility, reliability, perseverance, caution, thoughtfulness, practicality, hard work, and stability. Many Earth elementals become millionaires because of these traits.

AIR ELEMENT

The air element characteristic consists of yin or feminine traits. Air energy is associated with the qualities of care-free, kind-heartedness, trusting, independence, being optimistic, and pure joy.

WATER ELEMENT

The water element characteristic consists of yin or feminine traits. Water energy is associated with the qualities of mildness, flexibility, devotion, emotional, compassion, meditative, and creative.

METAL ELEMENT

This list of the most common elementals would not be complete without the metal element. Ancient Chinese Taoist scholars have added the metal element to represent the minerals, crystals, and gems of the world. It is comparable to the air element found in western traditions. The metal element energy consists of yin or feminine traits. Metal is associated with the qualities of persistence, strength, rigidity, determination, ambition, organization, and courage.

When you need these qualities of emotion or character traits, just call upon these elements of energy to help. They will be there to help you harness these energies for you or a client to portray when needed. For example, if you are going for an interview for a new job that requires stamina, you may want to call on the metal element. If you are going for an interview to be a screenwriter, you would want to call on the water element for creativity.

Yin/Yang; Female/Male Energies

When talking about the energies of male/female, it is interesting to know that these energies are related to geometric designs. Leonardo Da Vinci researched and dissected the geometric patterns of sacred geometry, wherein he found that energy patterns emerged that related to both male and female energies or yin/yang.

Female energies represented as a circle or a curve are more flowing. These energies are expressive and emotional. They can change their minds easily to go a different way, are very creative, think outside the box, and will look at the whole picture.

Whereas, a male's energies represented in a straight line are more practical, linear, strategic, focused, direct, to the point, and take direct roads going from Point A to Point B. These are energetic patterns created by Life Force Energy. Everything in the universe is geometric in design and so are we as Yin/Yang; male/female energies. I believe it is important to create a balance between the two energies to complete oneself energetically. Being able to pull the correct energy for your work, projects, or relationships can be beneficial to you.

Mother Earth's Energies

Mother Earth's energies consist of her soil, rocks, crystals, plants, and water. Each of these contains Life Force Energy and can hold and maintain Life Force Energy for long periods of time, perhaps millions of years. You can utilize the rocks, crystals, and all of Mother Earth's plants for healing. Her soil is used to sow, plant, and harvest to feed us from the abundance of crops.

Healing is about reconnecting to Mother Earth and utilizing her abundant resources. Many shamans use rocks and crystals and call upon their healing characteristic or traits. There are many books out there that can help you choose the stones or crystals that are right for you. After you are familiar with stones and crystals, then you will be ready to learn how to put together grids to manifest your desires to include healing.

An interesting story that happened to me personally is after my Mother passed away, I had to remain strong for the family. I was mainly in charge of all of the details and really stood strong for the family in their time of need. A few months afterwards, however, my spirit guides urged me to go for a walk in the local park and be among the trees. As I was walking through the park, I felt drawn to a large oak tree. As I stood before it, I knew that I needed to sit at its base with my back against the tree. Being November, the weather was a little chilly, but the sun was warm against my face as I sat and leaned against the tree's roots. There was a nice little place to sit on the roots of the tree and lean back snugly against the trunk. After about three minutes, my third eye chakra began to see the bright color of red. I could feel the strong energies of the tree going up my spine, from my root chakra all the way up to my crown chakra. The tree was giving *me* energy. It was a beautiful experience. However, that wasn't the last of my experience. As I relaxed even deeper into the tree, I saw in my third eye, bright white light coming out of the sky reaching into the branches of the tree. Wow! That was amazing! The white light came down the trunk of the tree and up my spine and stopped and filled my heart with beautiful blissful energies. A jolt of beautiful white light was opening my heart chakra. I began to weep and release the grief my heart had been carrying since my Mother's demise.

I am an empath, so I was able to feel the beautiful energies getting stronger. As the grief released from my heart, I felt pure bliss and joy. This is what Mother Earth can do for you. Trees, stones/crystals, and plants all have consciousness, I urge you to pay attention to them and learn their value.

Mother Earth's plants and herbs have also been used for thousands of years to make tinctures, essential oils, ointments, salves, etc. for healing your body. God has created these plants and herbs here on earth for a reason, and that is to help us with any ailment, including cancer. Essential oils have increased in popularity in recent years with aromatherapy because of its curative effects. However, essential oils have been in existence for a long time. They were created to help us be able to use the properties of the oil in making ointments, salves, etc. for healing and to allow us to store the usefulness of the plant longer. Essential oils may utilize the roots, leaves, and twigs, of the plants. Also, one of my favorites for healing emotions is the Bach Flower Essences created by Dr. Edward Bach in England. Powerful healings occur from the energies created by these plants.

Another Resource Mother Earth Provides Us

Where would we be on this planet if we didn't have water? Water is a vital part of our existence. Our bodies are made up of 70-80% water and without it, we would not survive. Therefore, it is important to keep our water supply healthy. Water is conducive to Life Force Energy as its molecules can change with the act of Blessing it. Holy Water is water that has been blessed by a minister or Holy man, and if you have pure God consciousness, so can you. Holy water has the ability to rid dark energies in homes, places, and/or land. (Please see Chapter 2.)

Energy cannot be created or destroyed.
It can only be changed from
one form to another.

– Albert Einstein

Chapter Eight

Ceremonial Dance, Energy Imprints, and Crystal Grids

Ceremonial Dance

Shamans and indigenous peoples throughout the world have known how to create and manifest through the powerful use of ceremonial dance that utilizes the natural law of attraction. They know how to tap into the earth's energies, spiritual beings, the spirit world, and are especially close to divine beings. This makes it relatively easy for them to manifest and create their desired outcome. Shamans also maintain the power and strength needed to gather Life Force Energy to manipulate weather patterns through the use of energy work.

The performance of ceremonial dances and/or rituals creates vortexes of energy in many places around the world. Even the tribes' thoughts and feelings have been imprinted into the world's atmosphere and Mother Earth wherever they reside.

In July of 2012, I had the pleasure of attending a Star Gate Activation spiritual ceremony at the ancient site of Serpent Mound in Peebles, OH. A Hawaiian elder by the name of Reynolds Nakooka Nahokualakaikawaikapuokalani, KAMAKAWIWOOLE 0' Kamehame conducted a ceremony to help restore Christ's Consciousness for the next 26,000 years, triple our spiritual levels through all dimensions, and to align and return humans to their pure Holiness. By calling in the ancient ancestors and by utilizing the powerful energies already present at Serpent Mound and within the universe, the people in attendance that day were responding with deep and powerful energies during the ceremony. It was a feeling of deep unconditional love and a beautiful intent of creation for the world.

It is with my profound thanks and gratitude that I was able to attend this beautiful ceremony. The group of over 40 healers in attendance left a powerful imprint of energy at Serpent Mound that day. Truly amazing healing went out to those who attended, including their families. It is without a doubt that as our years progress, we will find that more and more people, including spiritual leaders of this kind, will be doing more ceremonial and spiritual energy work to help heal the universe and those who live on this planet.

Other communities, cultures, and Tribal Nations have also included rituals and ceremonial dances in their communities because they work. Again, when you connect to God, you are praying and setting the intent for what you want to create and manifest.

Rituals set the tone for energy work to be done and the repetitiveness helps get the energy ready for what is about to happen. Ceremonies are our actions of dance and celebration to help us focus our intent to bring us into harmony with the universe and Life Force Energy. It is a time to celebrate and ask God for help with whatever we need help with. You can use the energy of the moon, sacred geometry, symbols, crystals, crystal grids, as well as the four directions (north, east, south, and west), and the five elements, ether, water, earth, fire, or air, in your ceremony because within these are the powers of all living things.

Plus, when you dance, you are moving your body and moving energy with each step. You are already working with Mother Earth's energies as well during dance rituals. The more you release during your dance—getting ego out of the way—the more energy you can move and the more you can manifest and create.

Energy Imprints

Energy imprints are an energy of something that is happening over and over again in the same space, place, and dimension. For example, when we prepare for bed, we are creating the same ritual every single night. This energy happens repeatedly in the same space. Therefore, an energy is being imprinted. This is the type of energy that can be left over in a house that has been inhabited by families before you. If there has been a murder in a house, the house will still hold the energy of that murder happening because it is a tragic event, and the energy will have been imploded with feelings and emotions tying it to the space. In homes where people have negative arguments all the time, the negative energy will be left behind in an energy imprint because of the energy of the arguments. The same holds true for positive happy families; the energy of happiness will be imprinted into the house.

Battlefields carry the energy of gunshots, cannon explosions, men crying in horror and pain where the energy was left behind. There is generally a lot of negative energy left behind in battlefields including the soldiers who died tragically on the battlefield. (See Chapter 11 for crossing over spirits.). Vehicle accidents also create energy imprints on our roadways. Accidents can generally be of such atrocity that the energy of the impact, emotions and feelings of the people are still left behind. The energy of people dying at the scene may still be there wondering what happened and not realizing they are dead.

On a more positive scale, you can create an energy imprint in entrances to hospitals, restaurants, stores, gas stations, or grocery stores, for whenever a person walks through that space/door. They will pass through an energy beam that has been imprinted into Mother Earth and reaches to Father Sky and then you can set the intent that whoever passes through that energy beam to give that person a corrective energy balance for their highest and best good.

In creating this energy imprinted vortex, all you need to do is connect to your choice of angel or ascended master. You can call in any number of angels or masters. It doesn't have to be just one. As you connect with them (See Chapter 3 for more information on these spiritual divine beings.), open your heart space, feel the flow of the angels and/or masters' energies surrounding you and ask for their protection. Create and set your intent as to what you want to manifest for that space. Now imagine in your mind that you are pulling energy up from the center of the earth, breathing in to the count of six slowly and take that energy up and out into the cosmos/universe as far out as you can take it. Then you will pull the energies back down from the universe to the count of six and place it back into the center of the earth. Repeat as many times as you feel is necessary to complete the vortex. Feel free to use sacred geometry to enhance your energy vortex or perhaps even create a crystal grid surrounding you in the space as you create the vortex. Be creative and send out as much love as possible for this world to be a happy, healthy, and lovely place to live. Here is an example, placed at the entrance of your home:

> *I call upon Archangel Raphael to surround me and keep me protected. Please be so kind as to create a space of joy and happiness so that every time anyone enters this home, their body will be cleansed and cleared of all negative energies. They will receive a blessing from God to be the best that they can be and receive unconditional love, peace, and happiness all the days of their life. Please keep them surrounded and protected in your light always.*
> *Thank you for your love and guidance. Amen.*

Now imagine pulling energies from the center of the earth and take them up to the Godhead, deep into the cosmos, all the time breathing in to the count of six. Then you can release the energy and pull down the Godhead energies from above back down into the center of Mother Earth (to the count of six seconds of breath). Repeat the energy pull for as long as you feel the energy is perfect for you. If you'd like, get the entire family involved and make it a family treat.

Crystal Grids

Not only do ceremonial and ritual dances create an abundance of happy energy, so do crystal grids. When you create a crystal and stone grid, you use your intent and focus along with the power of the stones to set a desired outcome. Creating grids is an ancient tradition for building energy for prayer, intent, and healing. Some examples of larger grids on the planet include Stonehenge, the Carnac stones in France, temples, the Montana Megalith sites in Montana, Punku in Machu Picchu, and the Bosnian and Egyptian pyramids. These powerful places still hold the memories and energy from many ceremonies of intention and energy building through the use of grids.

A person can manifest their desires or dreams with crystal grids, such as finding their soulmate, finding your life's purpose, attaining prosperity or abundance. You can also create better health for yourself or others. Use a grid to:

- raise your vibrations

- connect with angels, ascended masters, and spirits through higher meditation

- increase your psychic abilities

- protect your home

- ensure perfect restful sleep

- find overall inner peace and happiness

As you can see, the number of uses is endless. However, please remember that creating a grid should be used for you and/or someone else's highest and best good in mind. A grid is never to be used to make someone do something they do not want to do. Remember, you can lead a horse to water, but you can't make him drink. Everyone has a right to their own free will.

When making your grid, you can be as creative as you want with using other materials besides stones and crystals. Below is a short list of some of the things you can use in creating your grid.

- Symbols and sacred geometry

- Copper, silver & gold —all are conducive to energy

- Elements – fire, air, water, earth, ether

- Directions —north, south, east, west

- Color —use felt, colored paper or clothing

- Incense or candles

- Statues and/or totems – angels, animals, Buddha

- Numerology

Once you have determined what you want to manifest, you will need a location for the grid. You may want to create an altar and place it on a table or moveable tray. If you are sick, create the grid for healing and place it under your bed. If you are a healer or massage therapist, place a grid under your massage table for the perfect healing and/or balancing of all energies of your client and yourself. Place a grid in a garden for healthy fruits and vegetables or in your yard for protection. These are just a few suggestions. Be creative in your intent making process. Think about what it is you and your family need help with.

Now that you have found the perfect place, you will need to clear the space of any negative energies. The grid should be placed where it will not be disturbed. You will want to cleanse and clear your energies as well. The grid is going to be made with your energy and your intent, therefore, the clearer you are, the better. Use selenite or kyanite to sweep over your body to clear and cleanse any negative energy from yourself or use sage to smudge yourself and your space.

Now select crystals and stones based upon your intention for the grid. For example, if you wanted to connect with the higher angelic realm, you would want to use stones such as selenite, angelite, danburite, moldavite, etc. For creating a love relationship, you might use stones such as rose quartz, emerald, moonstone, lapis lazuli, or jade. These are just a few gemstones that are popular for their love properties. Be sure to do your research for the correct stones to use for the intent of your grid.

Once you have chosen the stones you want to use, you will need to cleanse them. You can clear your stones by various methods: 1) use your higher self and breath; 2) smudging; 3) set them out under the full moon energies overnight; 4) running water in a clear stream (not tap water) using the intent to clear (some stones don't like water so be careful with this one); 5) set them in herbs or incense to cleanse and clear; or, 6) set your stones on a selenite wand and wait ten to twenty minutes.

Now you will need to select a master crystal point for connecting your grid and cleanse it as well. It is important for you to use a crystal point that feels powerful to your energy to connect each of the stones in your grid.

Once all of your stones are cleared and ready to go, it's now time to program your crystals/stones. You will want to sit and meditate with all of your stones and use focused thought and intention in how you would like the stones to work for you. Do this for as long as it feels good. Take at least 20-30 minutes to set your intentions.

Here comes the fun part—putting it all together. This is where you can be as creative as you want. Place the crystals and stones in the space you have created for them. There is no wrong way to do this; just allow your intuition to flow. Once you have your stones set in the places you want, you will want to connect your stones together with your master crystal point. Point the master crystal toward each of the stones/crystals and connect them all together while you are thinking of your intent and how you want the grid to work for you. You can draw a master symbol, sacred geometry or call in your angels, guides, and ascended masters to help you.

Make this a very special time for yourself in this creation of powerful energies. Please express gratitude to the universe, angels, guides, etc. for helping you with manifesting your dreams and desires. The stones and crystals love to work with you, so be sure to have fun with it. Once your intention is achieved, you can take the grid down and clear all your stones and crystals. Be sure to express gratitude to your stones/crystals too.

The crystal grid pictured above presents a grid created for world peace. At the time, I didn't realize it was being created in the shape of the Tree of Life. The ascended masters were called in. The energies were allowed to create and manifest what the world needed at the time. I just followed along intuitively. The skull in the top center represents the hearts of the people in the world. The large skull in the center is made from amazonite and it represents hope. I used it to bridge our throat and third eye to our crown chakra. The stone citrine at the top with some grounding stones around it grounded it into Mother Earth—blue lace agate for communication, rose quartz for love, spirit quartz for universal love, pink howlite for balancing, and lepidolite for releasing old behavioral patterns, blue kyanite for cleansing and clearing our auric field, and balancing our chakras. Celestite was for uplifting vibrations and connecting us to our psychic abilities. The smaller points are diamantina crystal points that are used for bringing in energy of higher vibrational healing and attunements. Other points used are pink lemurian crystals that aid us in connecting higher to spirit and our spiritual evolution.

Everything in life is vibration.
Albert Einstein

CHAPTER NINE

Vibration, Sound Healing, Chakras and Colors, and Numerology

Vibration

We are vibrational beings, and as such, our vibration and/or frequency is our signature as to who we are and where we stand consciously. When we do meditations and leave our body, as in astral travel, others know us not by what we look like, but by our energy.

There are many books out there that speak about how vibration works in our bodies. There are meridians of energy that run up and down our bodies. The vibrational energy of our body slows down when we have emotional traumas. This emotion attaches itself to our body and changes our DNA. When we heal ourselves or when we go see a *healer of energy* we can release these emotions that plague us and, in turn, increase our vibrational energy in our bodies.

Why do you want to increase your vibrations? Increasing your vibrational frequency helps Life Force Energy to flow through your body with higher frequencies and therefore, it can potentially free you from disease.

The Golden Age is here and people are ascending into higher levels of consciousness. Being in the presence of awakened human beings will increase your vibrations. Even looking into the eyes of a saint or when viewing a picture or skype video of a higher spiritual or awakened being will increase your own vibrations. There will be a domino effect that more and more people will become awakened to spirituality as the vibrations of the earth and the people in it continue to raise their vibrations.

Sound also has a vibration to it. Using singing bowls, tuning forks, sound healing music with binary beats, or your own singing voice, can also increase a person's vibrations.

Meditation

Learning to meditate will increase your vibrations as well as place you in the alpha state of mind which can be used for healing practices. By practicing meditation, you set a goal to listen and when you are listening, it stops all the cluttered thinking in your life. It lowers your blood pressure, it allows you to relax, and it allows you to listen.

What are you listening for you ask? You can learn a lot about yourself. It helps you to slow down and think about what life is all about. Who are you? What do you need to do with your life? Is there anything you need to change about yourself or a situation that needs to be resolved? Would having a different job make you happier?

All of these questions can be answered only if we slow ourselves down and listen to ourselves and our spirit guides through meditation. Answers to questions will suddenly appear seemingly out of nowhere during meditation. These answers may be coming from your higher self or they may be coming from your spirit guides, angels, or God. Plus, if you set your intent prior to meditating, such as asking for a great night's sleep, that's exactly what you will get that night. Learn to work with and talk to your spirit guides daily.

To practice meditating, the first thing you want to do is to find that perfect time of day where you will not be disturbed by anyone. You should get at least 15 to 30 minutes of time by yourself. You can either sit up in an upright position in a chair with your feet flat on the floor, or your feet curled under your torso or in the lotus position. Personally, I find that 30 minutes prior to bedtime is when I like to meditate. It allows me to relax enough so that I can fall asleep easily afterward. And if you do fall asleep during meditation, no worries, it's what needed to happen. When I went to the Monroe Institute for a five-day retreat, most people fell asleep during the first two days of meditation because people generally don't get enough sleep. Do what feels best for you. It is a habit you will fall into once you find the right time of day and position that is best for you.

What I like to do when I begin meditating is to slow down my breathing. I do this by envisioning white light, and on a count of five I breathe in and envision white light coming up through my feet, up through my legs, up through my torso and then out the top of my head. Then I breathe out to a count of five, while envisioning white light going over the top of me and back down to my feet again. This allows me to focus on my breathing and guess what, the thoughts of the day simply melt away. This will also clear your chakras and balance your energy.

Now as you breathe in and out slowly to a count of five pay attention to relaxing the muscles in your feet, your arms, face, and body. Relax your body and take away all the frustrations of the day and release them. Let them go. Let your body relax. Listen only to music if you like and your breathing. I know you won't get it the first, second, or even third time around. However, with practice, you will find yourself learning how to control your breathing without thinking about it, as well as relaxing your body fully and completely.

When you meditate, your brain waves change. When you are fully coherent, your brain is utilizing beta brain waves. You are able to speak and think quickly. When you start a light meditation and slow yourself down, your brain will go into what's called, alpha waves. Theta stage is where healers should go automatically with practicing meditation. This is the trance state—a state of hypnosis. This is why meditation for people who do healing for others is so important.

When you practice meditation on a daily basis, you will find that when you start a healing session with someone you can automatically go into that trance state of theta waves almost immediately.

Attunements

Other ways to increase your vibrational energy patterns is through attunements. Attunements are a sacred initiation that will activate you in channeling increased levels of Universal Life Force Energies. Attunements will also support you in clearing out energy blockages and cellular memories that result from this lifetime, including past lifetimes. It allows for your body's vibration to be raised and your energetic system to be cleared, opening you up to channel higher levels of healing energy with the ability of carrying more light. Attunements will connect you more to your spiritual self and clear out karmic energy that is ready to be released. Negative energies don't release until you are ready and will enhance your sense of personal power. Attunements will greatly purify your body's system so you can be a strong conduit for God's healing energies helping you to heal yourself, your family, friends, pets, Mother Earth, and the cosmos.

Sound Healing

Because we are vibrational beings, it has been found through many years of test and trial that our body responds to the sound of our voice, crystal bowls, Tibetan vibrational bowls, music, tuning forks, etc. Sound healing has been researched by people such as Masaru Emoto, and The Monroe Institute.

As I talked about earlier in Chapter 5, Masaru Emoto of Japan discovered how water crystals change with music and different vibrations. It is clear through the pictures and research of Emoto that sound and thoughts can change the molecules of water. You can see the effect of thoughts and intent on the water. The negative thoughts created a substantial effect on the water wherein the crystals turned into a mucky looking substance. The research then turned to a Buddhist monk who prayed over the murky water for one hour, with the sound of his voice and his intention, it restored the water crystals back to their original state again.

With each type of music played in Mr. Emoto's research (for example, classical, heavy metal, and folk dancing music) the water crystals changed with each different type of music being played. The water crystals also changed with both positive and negative statements. Therefore, music and your own personal affirmations (what you think) can and does play a huge part in healing our bodies.

Again, it's good to reiterate that what we think, we create. This has a huge impact on our body and how well we are physically. When we think we are not good enough, happy enough, or loved enough, your body will respond to these thoughts and the vibration of your body will slow down and create illness.

To take it even further, Mother Earth is made up of roughly 70% water between the oceans, lakes, reservoirs and rivers, streams, glaciers, etc. Mother Earth can feel the effects of our negativity here on Earth. It's time we clean up our thoughts, feelings and language when it comes to both our bodies and the planet we live on.

The Monroe Institute in Virginia uses binary beats in their programs. The molecules of your body change because of the sounds of different tones being placed together (binary beats). The different frequencies of sound create different changes in the mind that affects the physical body. For over 60 years, the Monroe Institute has been researching the differences in various tones and what their functions are. I have had great success using sound healing in my energy practice with binary beats.

The body's defense against illness is our immune system. If our body is not working properly, it usually means that the energetic portion of our body is vibrating at a lower rate or speed. When our body is vibrating at a high level, it generally means that we are free from disease and that our energetic body is working properly.

Singing bowls, tuning forks, and your singing voice is also in the sound healing category. You can create and clear your healing space and heal yourself or others with the tone of your voice or sound from the vibrational singing bowl or tuning fork. The vibrations of your voice and/or bowl/tuning forks create a better vibration in the person you are healing, including yourself.

While visiting Mount Shasta, California, I met Gary Cromp, who was performing a sound healing. I didn't think much about it since I've done many crystal bowl healings, but my spirit guides were urging me to participate. I'm glad I listened. When I walked into the room, it was filled with crystal bowls and large apparatuses that were concocted from copper and metal piping to solfeggio crystal bowls and a crystal harp. There were crystals attached to most of the handmade devices that sound would emanate from. He indicated to the group that participated that day that he was downloaded with the information that would create these beautiful sounds and tones of frequency. The bowls and handmade devises covered a 500-square-foot room. There were two people performing the sound.

Durng the one-and-a-half hour group healing session, my body responded from deep within my sacral chakra and brought emotions of profound release to the surface through the form of tears. I could feel this energy working its way up my body and out. Sound and frequency is instrumental in healing your physical body—one more way of helping our body to dive deeply into those emotions held within.

Chakras and Colors

The first book I ever read in the metaphysical field was on chakras. To tell you the truth, I was in over my head. I had no clue what a chakra was, I even laughed out loud and thought, "Man, these people are crazy." However, since then I have found out differently. If you are just starting out, I would say be patient with yourself. It takes time to learn this and how it all comes together.

The word chakra comes from the Sanskrit word that means wheel or turning. Chakras are a person's energy centers that give and receive energy at all times of the day and night. Since chakras draw or pull energy to us, there are times we are picking up other people's energies and emotions that we come into contact with. Having balanced chakras, your body will be healthier and be more in tune with yourself.

When a person's chakra is closed, it means that very little energy is flowing to and from that part of the body. Think of a chakra as a vortex (a mini tornado) of energy flowing in and out of certain parts of your body. According to Barbara Brennan in her book, *Hands of Light*, there are a total of 132 chakras in your body, but only seven are major chakras. They are located mainly throughout your spine starting at the root chakra which is located at the very end of your tailbone and working its way up to your crown chakra which is at the top of your head.

The following lists the colors associated to each chakra, where it's located in the body, and a little about its function:

ROOT CHAKRA

Located at the very end of your spine closest to your legs, the first is associated with the reproductive glands (testes in men and ovaries in women). It controls sexual development and secretes sex hormones.

The color associated with the root chakra is red. This chakra has to do with stability, financial stability, being grounded, survival-oriented, courage and action, and passion.

Fifth dimension color – pearl-white light.

SACRAL CHAKRA

Two inches below the belly button and associated with the adrenal glands, it regulates the immune system and metabolism.

The color associated with the sacral chakra is orange. This chakra will free fertility, creativity, sexuality and emotions. Hence the reason that when you feel emotion and you get that gut feeling about things, your sacral chakra is working on your behalf.

Fifth dimension color – pink-orange light.

SOLAR PLEXUS CHAKRA

Associated with the pancreas, it regulates metabolism. It is located about one inch above your naval or belly button.

The color associated with the solar plexus is yellow. This chakra represents our identity, or how we see and feel about ourselves. It is where your self-esteem, self-confidence, will power, and a sense of responsibility comes from.

Fifth dimension color – golden light.

HEART CHAKRA

The heart chakra is in the center over your chest where your heart is. Associated with the thymus gland; it regulates the immune system.

The color associated with the heart chakra is green, and it relates to heart and lungs. It allows us the ability to give and take love unconditionally. When this chakra is balanced, we can give love and also can love and nurture ourselves. It also cleanses and balances our energy that gives us peace and harmony. Green connects us to unconditional love and is used for balancing our entire being.

Fifth dimension color – violet-pink light.

THROAT CHAKRA

By its location, it is associated with the thyroid gland, upper lungs, and respiratory system; it regulates body temperature and metabolism. The throat chakra is at your Adam's apple in the center of your throat.

The color associated with the throat chakra is light blue. When this chakra is balanced, you have the ability of hearing, speaking, listening and communicating. It is the area of the body where your communication abilities emerge, and is associated with hearing, including psychic hearing (clairaudience).

Fifth dimension color – deep blue-violet light.

THIRD EYE CHAKRA (BROW CHAKRA)

Associated with the pituitary gland, it produces hormones and governs the function of other glands. The third eye chakra is located at the center of your forehead.

The color associated with the third eye chakra is indigo blue. This chakra is directly related to your senses of psychic sight, hearing, and intuition. It has to do with how we see the world we live in and our perception of it (our wisdom). Balancing this chakra can help remove confusion and increase your ability to see clearly to make important decisions.

Fifth dimension color – golden-white light.

CROWN CHAKRA

The final one is associated with the pineal gland and regulates biological cycles, including sleep. The crown chakra is located on the top of the head.

The color associated with the crown chakra is lavender or white. When this chakra is open and functioning properly, it becomes an open doorway through which higher spiritual knowledge is received along with full enlightenment and union with the cosmos.

Fifth dimension color – violet-white light.

As I have mentioned in each of the seven categories above, there is a color and gland associated with each chakra. Each chakra has a different vibration to it in accordance to the color it represents. For example, red is the slowest in vibration, and it creates the longest wavelength, whereas, violet has the fastest vibration and is the shortest wavelength.

If you have a chakra that you believe may be closed or not rotating well enough, you can wear the color of that chakra on your body to help open that chakra. (Be sure to be checked by a medical doctor if problems persist.). Even wearing chakra-colored jewelry or having chakra-colored stones close to you will also help you open your chakras. For example, if you are in marketing, you would want to communicate well and be effective. Therefore, wearing anything light blue will help your throat chakra to open and work well for you. You can also eat fruits and vegetables associated with the colors of the chakras to help open your chakras. For example, eating root vegetables such as beets, potatoes, turnips, carrots, etc. helps your root chakra.

Pink is the color of unconditional love; therefore, if you want to draw love to you, wear pink. If you want to feel grounded and stable, wear the color red to help you. Some people who have Air Element qualities sometimes need help with being grounded and so wearing black or red could help them a lot.

Numerology

Numerology is the study of numbers and learning about how the energy and vibration of those numbers influence our daily lives. Pythagoras, who was a famous Greek mathematician and philosopher, believed that individual numbers hold energy and vibration to them. He felt that each individual's birth date and name held vibrations and that we could understand ourselves and others better by understanding what the meaning is of each number's vibration. In addition to our birthdays and names containing these vibrations, our house numbers, towns and states where we live or have lived, all hold vibrations and can become challenging to our personal being.

For example, my house number at a time in my life that I needed strength and endurance was 7183. To find the vibration of this house number, you add together 7+1+8+3 = 19 and then reduce that down (9+1= 10) to the number one.

A little story to go with this example, is when I was looking for a house, I had chosen a house two doors down. Unfortunately, I didn't get that house. Someone else moved there. I chose another house and with that house, I was approved and moved in shortly thereafter. This was at a time when I was newly divorced and had just started a business of my own.

The number one vibration and energy is the angels and ascended masters telling you the time is good to manifest your desires. It has the attributes of independence, ambition, leadership, and new beginnings. This number also carries with it the vibrations of masculine characteristics of organization, achievement, success, strength, self-reliance, tenacity, and love. This was the epitome of my life at that time so having the number one vibrational energy as my address helped me through new beginnings and creating a strong business for myself. The other address was 7167, which added together is, 7+1+6+7= 21. When reduced: 2+1=3. The number 3 energies are inspiration, creativity, speech, imagination, and communication. At the time, I needed the number one energy instead of the three energies to help hold me up and provide a strong foundation for me and my business.

This is just a short synopsis of how number vibrations and their energies can and will affect your life. I highly suggest finding a great book on numerology to find out where you are on your journey.

Because one believes in oneself, one
doesn't try to convince others.
Because one is content with oneself, one
doesn't need others' approval.
Because one accepts oneself, the whole
world accepts him or her.

- Lao Tzu

Mary Bannon

Chapter Ten

Different Healing Modalities

As you have read in the previous chapters, there are many ways to tap into Life Force Energies. Our mind is a very complex and complicated piece of work. Because of that, we are always reaching for goals rather than being in the experience of the *now* or *present* moment. We are also powerful beings when we can focus our minds. Focused thoughts create miracles. Furthermore, when we focus our minds to our *now moment* and *reality*, we then are limited only by our beliefs. If you can believe it, you can achieve it. If we believe all things are possible, we can choose our own possibility, our own reality.

The qualities of being a master of energy are:

- compassion

- detachment

- non-judgment

- clarity

- composure

- service

- love

All of these qualities are important for living a good spiritual life. Every one of us is on a journey to expand and raise our consciousness. Although keep in mind, we are not in a race to beat the other person. Go at your own pace. With every moment we are experiencing and recording it into our being, into our soul. We are learning lessons every step of the way. If you look at every thought we have as a prayer, would you clean up your thoughts a little better? Every moment you experience—along with the emotions and feelings—you are sending these messages to your body, to the universe itself, into your daily reality, relationships, and the world, especially, the mass collective. Why would anyone want to chase after the low vibing conspiracy theories? We all have a right to know what's going on in the world. Use your intuition and wisdom that comes from the universe for your answers.

Compassion

What does it take for a person to be compassionate? Ask yourself if you are without a hidden motive when you are doing something for someone else. Are you judgmental when it comes to others? Where does your ego lie?

You must ask yourself these questions as to where your heart is. Are you helping others just to feel important?

The thing I want you to think about is where is your heart in the matter? Are you compassionate? In order to achieve compassion, one must not be judgmental or place their ego above others. One must feel compassion for others in their heart space.

Detachment

One must also be detached from the outcome of the intention being presented. For example, you want the person to be healed so badly that your feelings to make the person better are overwrought with your own ego. Ego takes over your heart and the focused intention falls apart. In God's eyes, there may be a different plan for the person you are trying to heal. There could be a better plan. Letting go and letting God is my motto here. Have the confidence that you can change and perform alchemy and then get your ego out of the way for healing to happen.

Nonjudgmental

Being judgmental actually brings your consciousness down. Is ego involved when we judge another? Are you jealous? What are your motives? Being in the moment and being nonjudgmental shows your integrity. Being without judgement for another's choices keeps your consciousness level high.

Clarity

Being able to focus the mind on a certain aspect of what you want changed is needed to be a master of energy. If your energy or mind is not focused on the outcome of what it is that you want, how can the universe provide it?

Composure

Composure is a needed aspect because you need to be calm, relaxed, and focused on the given subject of what you are changing.

Service

When you tell the universe that you are willing to help in any way possible, then you are in service to others. Your help can be as little as a prayer, but I think you know just how powerful that is. When you do that, you are telling the universe that you are in service to helping others in need.

Love

One must also have love in their heart for if they don't have love, they have nothing.

1 Corinthians 13:2 New King James Version.
And though I have the gift of prophecy, and under-
stand all mysteries, and all knowledge; and though
I have all faith, so that I could remove mountains,
and have not love, I am nothing.

Couple all these qualities with your emotional body such as feelings, love, and compassion, and then you have just created a miracle with your prayers and intentions.

My experience with energy work has grown so much over the years that my thoughts, feelings, and my heart create miracles when working with others' energy fields. My heart vibrates now on a continual basis with a higher vibration. I am not telling you this to boast. I am explaining that the heart is the key of the matter when it comes to performing miracles when helping others to heal.

John 14:12 in the New Heart English Bible:
Truly, truly, I tell you, he who believes in me, the
works that I do, he will do also; and he will
do greater works than these, because I
am going to the Father.

What is Reiki

Usui Reiki was created by a Japanese man by the name of Mikao Usui in the 1800s who climbed to the top of Mount Kurama to meditate on how to help others heal. After 21 days of meditation and fasting on the mountain, he learned his answers of using Life Force Energy along with different symbols to create and manifest healing. Reiki is an alternative healing practice where you learn to tap into Life Force Energy and use it for healing your energetic body with the use of symbols and channeling Life Force Energy from the universe to be given to the recipient. However, in 1994, the original manuscript of Usui states the practice originated from Gautama Buddha. In either case, Reiki has become a mainstream norm.

Reiki has become quite popular over the years and because of this, doctors and chiropractic offices all over the world are beginning to treat the whole person (mind, body, and *spirit*) instead of just the body and utilizing some form of energetic treatment. You can also incorporate other treatments with Reiki, such as essential oils, binary beat music, sound therapy, crystal healing, Integrated Energy Therapy ® IET (angel healing), 2Points 2Freedom (quantum physics), and many others.

Usui Reiki is a modality wherein the teacher will attune the student to receive the ability to perform this task. Each time a student is attuned to Reiki, it will release negative energies in that person and raise the student's vibrational energy and turn on their ability to use Life Force Energy through channeling the energy through their body and into the recipient.

There are three levels to Reiki, Level I is for the person to work on healing themselves. Level II is to train people to treat others, and Level III, Master/Teacher Level, is to teach more knowledge about energy work, as well as teaching methods to students for them to teach others.

What is Integrated Energy Therapy (IET) ®

IET is a healing modality that utilizes angels to help heal your body. In the 1980s, Steven Thayer founded IET with the help of Archangel Ariel who channeled information to him about how to clear the physical body from traumatic emotional feelings our bodies hold onto including our aura or field of energy surrounding our bodies.

Steven had practiced as a Reiki Master but found that Reiki did not release all of his clients' personal emotional traumas. He learned that by connecting your heart to the heart of the angels and then connecting your heart to your clients, you become a channel for the angels' energies. Using the techniques provided in this modality of healing, your emotional trauma from this life or past lives is lifted from your body at integral points on your body that holds trapped emotions.

With this modality, the teacher will attune the student to the angelic energies as part of this training and receive a higher level of DNA activation. To be clear, when performing this modality as a trained practitioner, after the negative energy is released, you then channel the angels' energies into your client. At that time in my life, I had no idea the body's energy fields held onto so much emotional baggage. After I had my first session, I felt the energies I had been holding onto being pulled and released out of my body. Then, I felt the higher vibrational energies of the angels filling my body with their pure white light; I became a total believer.

Trust me, I needed personal healing because of my historical past of living with an alcoholic husband. If anyone reading this has ever lived with an alcoholic, you know that sometimes they can be demeaning and literally tear apart your self-esteem. My healing came when my IET practitioner got to the place on my body that represents victimization.

Even though I had been victimized by my husband for years, I had forgiven him and all the rotten mean-spirited things he ever did to me. However, my physical body was holding onto the actual emotional trauma I went through. My fears were released that day as well. I got to feel the great powerful energies of Archangel Michael releasing my fears. This was a healing of a lifetime, a beautiful moment to experience and remember forever.

To date, as a practitioner of IET, I have had many magical healings. To give you an example, when a person has been hurt from the breakup of a relationship, IET will clear your heart from the sadness and emotional damage that relationship left you with. The angels will replace it with their unconditional loving energies. I have people tell me all the time that they feel unconditional love for the very first time in their life because of the angels' energies filling them up with their unconditional love. It truly is amazing. It is called a miracle in the truest sense of the word.

THE FOLLOWING ARE A FEW EXPERIENCES FROM MY PRACTICE OF IET:

I was providing holistic healing at a local psychic fair wherein I met a beautiful young lady in her 30s, who came to the fair to receive a psychic reading. Unfortunately, she was having a lot of problems with men because of her beauty. She truly was a stunningly beautiful young lady. After her reading, the psychic suggested she have an IET healing with me, and she agreed. The minute I placed my hands on her, I knew she had been molested at an early age by a male family member. This set the tone for the rest of the healing. She was currently in a court battle because her ex-boss, a respected physician in the community, had made numerous sexual advances toward her. This is what she has had to live with her entire life. Her fears of men were paramount, so much so, her feelings of hatred of men were coming through me, and my body was releasing her trauma. I was literally crying my eyes out. This session was the first experience of this nature for clearing out so much emotional trauma. During the session, with the help of Archangel Michael, we were able to release the emotional trauma of what men have done to her in this lifetime. It was a very uplifting experience for both of us to know she won't forget about this abuse while her body was able to release the trauma. Therefore, she is now able to live a freer life. She is no longer attached to the dogma of her trauma.

Another miraculous healing happened with the son of an alcoholic father who had restricted his communication and his ability to move forward in life. During the healing session, this man's body literally lifted up off of the massage table and his hips moved up and then back down. You could see the organs under his skin and ribs moving into their rightful place. He told me later he had been having problems with his hips for two years and his chiropractor was not able to put them back into place, but IET and the angels healed him that day. He is now able to speak his truth about his life, as well as, move forward without the emotional trauma his body had held onto. He now has a new feeling of freedom and feels like he can finally be himself.

If you are interested in learning more about IET, please visit my website at www.divineheartconnections.com or go to www.learniet.com.

Akashic Records

Akashic records are the informational energy surrounding

your body that have been recorded and maintain all of the information from every life you have ever lived including potential lives you will live in the future. You can and have tapped into your Akashic records when you have had feelings like you've been someplace before or by seeing repeat patterns of something you do over and over again. For example, when I watched the movie *Dances with Wolves,* I found myself very attracted to the movie as though I myself had lived during that time period in the Great Plains married to a White man with me being the Indian woman. As I write this, my spirit guide is confirming for me that I did indeed live a lifetime as a Cheyenne Indian. During an energy session once, I had a vision of a lifetime being a Native American and found that my spirit guide today was my brother from that lifetime. During this energy session, I was tapping into my Askasha and my records.

If you are an energy practitioner, you too can tap into your client's Akashic records during healing sessions, with their permission of course, to help them heal from past lives and with the help of the Akashic record keeper, angels, healing and spirit guides. When you are stating your opening prayer for protection and calling in your guides, angels, and ascended masters for the healing, just ask the Akashic record keeper to open the person's records for their highest and best good for healing. Your intent for healing the person must come from your compassion and foremost your heart for the Akasha to be opened.

Intelligent Body

In the past few years, I have had the opportunity to experience other modalities of healing that utilize your body to determine what it needs to heal. For example, I have had sinus problems throughout my life. Recently, I found out it had to do with how I responded and reacted to the trauma of living with an alcoholic husband. In other words, my anger toward my ex-husband was the cause of my sinus condition. My body was holding onto all that anger. When we live in a life full of turmoil, our body system reacts to protect itself, causing numerous problems in our system because of the breakdown of energy flow and energy patterns that develop.

My grandmother, who passed at the age of nearly 101, was always sick as a child. She was raised with a sister who needed more attention as she had epilepsy. It makes sense that when she was growing up she saw that when you are sick, you receive attention. This is the only reason her intelligent body was sick. She was looking for attention. The next time you are sick, please take a look at your lifestyle. Are you too busy? Is life hectic and your body is getting sick to make you slow down? Do you feel left out and need attention from others? My grandmother eventually grew out of that attention-getting somatic psyche and was never ill unless she wanted to be.

For the sake of simplicity, your body is extremely intelligent. Think about it, if your body is made up of 70-80% water molecules and some matter, and energy is conducive to water, then your body is absorbing everything.

Your body also responds to you as though it has a brain and/ or a consciousness. Perhaps every organ in your body has this same consciousness. Why not? After all, your body is listening to everything you think, say, or do. For example, when I make a statement to my body, it responds by healing itself. You can do this for yourself or if you have a client, use positive statements by talking to your body, such as, "My body is in perfect health." "I am completely healthy." Plus, seeing yourself as a perfect being with no issues such as arthritis, high blood pressure, or whatever the ailment may be, will allow your body to respond in a positive way.

It makes sense to mention here that this goes both ways. There are hypochondriacs who are always worried about illness wherein they are creating their reality.

Two-Point Method

When you tap into Life Force Energy, there is a way to also tap into quantum fields, morphic fields, wormholes, and electromagnetic fields, as a direct link to God. The objective of using the two-point method is to provide a simple and gentle way to open the door for healing to happen.

The two-point method is a very old method that has been a tradition of Hawaiian Shamans by the name of Kahi or Ahi which means oneness. This method is a very simple way to unblock and release the flow of energy. The healing happens when you simultaneously connect two points in a person's body or energy field. The positive effects of the two-point method are felt immediately within your body as physical or emotional and sometimes energetically.

You can heal relationships, stop overeating, quit smoking, stop pain, remove allergies, the list is endless. All you need to do is believe that you can. Because of the way you were raised, you may be in the same situation I was in myself, believing this type of healing is the craziest thing you have ever heard of. Keep an open mind and practice on yourself every day, and you will find that it truly does work.

I have learned many different energy modalities, and I have found this one to be the simplest and easiest way to change energetic patterns easily and effortlessly. Some people may call this a quantum energy technique or even quantum touch healing. However, learning to use this modality daily will help you in all areas of your life.

For example, when you schedule an interview for a new job, two-point yourself to help you relieve your stress to be calmer. If you are selling your house, two-point the energy around your house to make it the most noticeable and sellable house in your area, and then two-point the buyers to pay the amount you want to sell it for. This energy modality can and will transform your life.

Should you have interest in learning this modality, just check out my website www.divineheartconnections.com to see where I will be teaching it in your area.

Crystal Healing

Crystal healing is a form of healing through the use of crystals and stones. My spirit guides told me they could help me more if I used crystals and stones during healing sessions. Stones hold energy and can help change our energy by placing it on or near our body.

When quartz crystals are programmed, it can raise your consciousness toward enlightenment and can purify you on all levels. Quartz will amplify energy and your intentions. Being programmable, quartz crystals can hold a program much longer than other minerals. Be sure to use them as an activator in grids to set your intent for the highest healing for everyone who enters your healing room. You can also set the intent that the archangels program the crystal/stone for you and all you have to do is set the stone in the proper place on the area that needs to be healed.

Before we begin, let me repeat myself here: do what you think is correct for you. If your intuition says to use pink when you were taught to use green, use your own judgment; listen to *your* intuition. Since you will be calling your guides in to help, listen to them. Be sure to get into the zone of theta state that you have been practicing with meditation.

First you will want to clear the space and seal it for the highest good by envisioning lines going from each corner of the room and then coming together in the center of the room. Take several deep breaths to relax and concentrate on opening your heart space. Then call in your ancient ancestors, God, your healing/spirit guides, archangels, and ascended masters. Ask them to surround and protect both you and your client. Also ask them to guide you and direct you for the highest healing for the client. You are now connected to the highest realms of spirit.

If you want to create a shortcut for contacting and calling in your entourage of healing angels for preparation of a healing session, first, you will need a symbol of some sort that tells your healing guides that every time you show them a symbol on a piece of paper or envision the symbol in your third eye, you are calling them in to begin your session. You create it; you do what is right for you. It's just a shortcut to call them in. You should still utilize prayers for protection.

The next thing you should do is to make sure your client is completely comfortable, in terms of the temperature of the room, a pillow for their head, perhaps a blanket for warmth or even a bolster for their legs, along with some soft music.

Now you are ready to begin. Take a blue kyanite wand, start at the head and act as if the wand were a knife cutting through your client's auric field. Hold the wand about two inches above the body. Start at the head and move the wand through the air all the way down past their root chakra, or to their legs. Please do not touch the client with the wand.

Kyanite is a stone that never needs cleansing. It is a powerful and high vibrating stone that can align a person's chakra in minutes. You can use orange or green kyanite as well. However, I have found that blue kyanite works the best for me, and it is easily available to purchase.

Now take the blue kyanite wand and rotate in a spiral pattern to the right over each chakra to allow the chakra to spin correctly. Use as many rotations needed to move the energy properly. Use your intuition here. Start at the root chakra, moving your way upward through the sacral, solar plexus, heart, throat, third eye, and ending with the crown. You start with the root chakra to keep your client rooted and grounded.

The next step is to take a quartz laser wand, a crystal that your energy is strong with. The wand can be a lemurian seed crystal, diamantine laser, rutilated quartz point, or a crystal point—whichever one that works best for you. Repeat the process of rotating the wand in a clockwise motion, starting at the root chakra, rotate the wand about three inches above each chakra.

Take your hand, place palm down about three inches above the person's chakra to feel (use your clairsentience) how open or closed that chakra is. You may need to continue the circular clockwise motion above each chakra until you are satisfied with the movement of energy going in and out of the chakra you are working on. If you cannot feel energy move yet, you can use a pendulum above each chakra to see how the energy is moving.

When you are satisfied with each chakra, take the wand and start at the feet. Wave the wand from foot to head in a sweeping motion back and forth across the body from head to toe, not touching the person's body. This will allow the wand to absorb any negative energies you have just pulled from the body and help the client's body to balance itself out.

If you feel any more negative energies in their body, you can take one hand and place it near the client's heart, not touching them. Take the laser wand, point the smallest end of the quartz outwards, and imagine drawing out all negative energies from the person's body. Imagine the negative energy flowing into the room and bursting into a golden white light.

Now start placing the appropriate stones on each of the chakras.

Root Chakra – red jasper

Sacral Chakra – carnelian

Solar Plexus Chakra – tiger eye

Heart Chakra – rose quartz or green aventurine

Throat Chakra - blue lace agate

Third Eye Chakra - lapis lazuli or sodalite

Crown Chakra - amethyst or blue celestite

These listed are only suggestions and my personal favorites. However, you can research and utilize your own. Please feel free to use the stone you feel will provide the best results for the clients' highest and best good. Utilizing your intuition and trusting it helps you grow.

Using clear quartz points on each chakra also works well. If you want to get creative, place a drop of essential oil, representative of each chakra, on the quartz. I will place a list at the end of this chapter for you to refer to for the best results.

If you have another modality of treatment that you work with (i.e., two pointing, Reiki, IET, etc) you may perform these treatments at this time for your client.

After your healing treatment, you can remove the stones from your client. Start at the head and work your way down to the bottom ending with the root chakra. You do this to keep the person as grounded as possible with the jasper left in place. There may be times when the stones fall off the client. Don't worry about it, as the stone has completed its task.

Next, take a selenite wand and sweep it over your client's body from head to toe in long sweeping motions until you feel that all negativity has been captured. Selenite is a great stone to have in your home, office, and healing room as it absorbs negativity, plus it never needs to be cleansed.

It is always my ritual to be grateful for the wonderful miracles that happen with every healing. Please take the time now to thank your energy guides, angels, ascended masters, loved ones, and spirit guides for their loving support and help after each session.

Please ground your client and yourself afterward. Stand at your client's feet and hold their ankles down gently while envisioning a pink blanket of positivity being pulled over their body. You can use black tourmaline essential oil on the bottoms of your client's feet to help ground them. You can also use a black tourmaline stone—just place it in their hands. Once they sit up, have them place their right hand on their left knee and their left hand on their right knee. However, please, feel free to use whatever works best for you and your client. Please do not allow your client to leave and/or drive until they feel they are grounded and back in their body.

You will want to cleanse your stones after each use by whatever means you have been taught and by what your intuition tells you to do. Here are a few suggestions I like to use.

- Blow with your Sacred breath—your higher self surrounded in white light—into your crystals for cleansing.

- Place your crystals and stones on top of a selenite wand for at least 10 to 20 minutes.

- Sage your stones.

- Place them in the ground outside in your garden for several hours.

- Cleanse them in the sun or full moon light, taking great care if the stone is sensitive to fading in the sun.

Using Essential Oils on Chakras

If you find a chakra is having a hard time opening, you could use a clear crystal point with some essential oil on the crystal and place the crystal on the person's chakra. Please, be sure that the crystal has been properly cleared before using. By using essential oils on a crystal—ideally a quartz crystal—we can open and re-align a closed or partially closed chakra with only one drop of essential oil on the crystal. I have created my own blend of essential oils that I currently use for each chakra. However, the following is an outline of pure essential oils that can be used on the seven major chakras easily and effectively.

Ist chakra - Root-
Use myrrh, patchouli or cedarwood

2nd chakra – Sacral
Use jasmine or ylang-ylang

3rd chakra – Solar plexus
Use ginger, lemon, or rosemary

4th chakra – Heart
Use rose, thyme, or bergamot

5th chakra – Throat
Use sandalwood, neroli, or frankincense

6th chakra – Third Eye
Use juniper, rosemary, or patchouli

7th chakra – Crown
Use vetiver, myrrh, or sandalwood

*Note: lavender can be used for all chakras.

I have used all the above practices with great success. I wish you well in your endeavors for healing and continuing to heal yourself and others.

Frequency of Light and the Seven Rays

Some of my favorite experiences are working with the energy of the Twelve Rays of God as explained in *The Complete Ascension Manual, How to Achieve Ascension in This Lifetime* by Joshua David Stone, Ph.D. His explanation is that every human being on earth is made up of six different rays. We are a portion of each of the energies of these rays that were created by God. You could see them as "personalities." Just as we can call in animal totems and the energy of animals, so can we bring in these rays of light from God to bring in an energy or "personality of an energy." Stone's information was derived from the Alice Baily books. For more detail on this subject, please see the books: *Esoteric Psychology, Volumes One and Two*, and *The Rays and the Initiations*. I will have to say that there are many interpretations into these rays, but I will do my best to give you a very basic understanding here. Each of these rays brings forth into the human soul characteristics and personalities within each, depending on whether they are pulling from the soul's higher expression or lower expression of self.

Each of these rays is a type of energy that you can call upon the resources to possess. First I will give you a short synopsis of each ray and its meaning.

RAY I—WILL OR POWER

The color is red. People with this ray have a strong sense of power and they are not afraid to use it. This ray can be used for good or evil. A small portion of this energy will suffice. This energy is of power, drive, and a person's strong will. This ray will intensify any condition or energy that already exists. You could consider a person who possesses this ray "a born leader," a military man or policeman. Should a person be traumatized, this ray of energy could be used to "pull themselves out of the trauma" with strength and endurance. Every person could use a little of this ray just for confidence building. Wearing the color red will bring about its attributes and energy. The downside of this ray is someone who tries to manipulate and control you. A person who possesses too much of this type of energy could be so fearless that they die for their cause unwittingly. People with this ray start wars and are not afraid to fight the battle. They can also have too much pride, arrogance, anger, and obstinance.

RAY II—LOVE AND WISDOM

The color of this ray is blue. People who embody this type of energy are very loving, considerate, friendly, and responsible. This ray brings about vulnerability, compassion, unselfishness, and sensitivities. This type of person would be a great ambassador, school teacher, or head of a college. Great world ascended masters were of this ray—Kuthumi, Maitreya, and Buddha to name a few. When you wear the color blue, it brings in a calmness, strength, patience, and endurance. Some of the lower aspects of this ray may bring a person to be overdramatic in their studies and unable to process cognitively why another person is limited mentally.

RAY III—ACTIVE INTELLIGENCE AND POWER TO MANIFEST

The color of this ray is yellow. People with this particular ray are thinkers, philosophers, and metaphysicians. They are excellent at math and have a high imagination. They can be idealistic dreamers. A main characteristic of a Ray III personality is perseverance. They hold the ability to finish projects through to the end. They are generally on a spiritual path working to find the truths to matters. Wearing the color yellow may bring about perfectionism, focus, and clear mindedness. Issues a third ray personality may be inflicted with are coldness, pride, isolation, and selfishness.

RAY IV—HARMONY THROUGH CONFLICT

The color of this ray is emerald green. Those with this personal energy are always fighting polarity between the higher and lower expressions. They are always trying to find a balance. This ray is also associated with people who are very driven in the arts of music, dance, and painting. The fourth ray people have a tendency to get too emotional in their energy and have highs and lows. People in the past who have demonstrated this type of energy are Mozart, Leonardo da Vinci, Picasso and Van Gogh. The downsides of this ray are manic-depression, lack of moral courage, worrying, and perhaps self-centeredness as they feel everyone should believe in what they believe in. The upside of this ray and personality is sympathy, courage, and generosity because they are often in their emotional body. Emotions are, after all, feelings.

RAY V—CONCRETE MIND

The color of this ray is orange. People who demonstrate this energy ray are very truthful, have an expanded knowledge base, and are factual. One with this type of energy is not generally open to their intuition as they are very scientifically based. However, they do have the ability to access the higher mental body which is the realm of the soul. The qualities found in a fifth ray person are connections to "new thought" in New Age Churches as they are seeking the truth of the matter in everything. The downfall for fifth ray personalities is arrogance, lack of sympathy, and unforgiveness. When bringing in this ray of energy, you feel a cold and heavy energy.

RAY VI—DEVOTION AND IDEALISM

The color of this ray is indigo. This ray is someone who completely immerses themselves in religion. People with this energy are very emotional and need to devote themselves to a deity or personal god. Religious wars and crusades have been based on the energy from this ray. Some people are so absolutely devoted to their cause that they seem almost possessed. Due to our higher evolution at this stage, this ray is moving out of existence as it doesn't serve a purpose any longer. Humanity has matured enough that this ray is no longer useful. Anger, jealousy, selfishness and prejudice are some of the many vices of this ray.

RAY VII—CEREMONIAL ORDER AND MAGIC

The color of this ray is violet as it is associated with the violet flame of transmutation and Saint Germain. People who are able to manipulate energy are privy to this ray as the high priest/priestess. Saint Germain is an ascended master and responsible for developing the Golden Age on earth. This ray is incredible in that it is integrating heaven and earth, as well as grounding spirituality into the world. The type of person who possesses this ray always wants to do the right thing—white magic, a mindset of unity, creating rituals and ceremonies to move energy. They are always fluent in writing and speech. The seventh ray person is in service to and works directly with God. The lower expression of this energy is judgment, pride, and bigotry.

Each person may reflect a certain percentage in a combination of these rays. Not all people are alike in that respect. However, each person has the ability to call in which energetic ray they want to work with at any given time.

As the humans on this planet continue to grow spiritually and release the toxins of pain known throughout eternity, our planetary system here on earth has been given new higher-frequency rays. In the early 1970s, the planet was able to reach into the fourth dimension of working on ourselves. It was imperative these new rays reach us and allow us to utilize their powers. The new rays are created with Source light and are the ones that I use more predominantly in healing sessions.

RAY VIII—HIGHER CLEANSING RAY

The color of this ray is seafoam green. It is an incredible ray to help people move out of the qualities within that they no longer want to embody. This light is great for clearing out the subconscious mind of pre-programming and PTSD trauma. Once you have cleared the four-body system with this ray, you can move onto the next ray.

RAY IX—JOY, ATTRACTION OF THE BODY OF LIGHT

The color of this ray is blue-green. This ray brings much joy into your bodily system. This ray is responsible for bringing in one's fullest potential, as well as continuing the healing process created by the eighth ray. It is used to attract the body of Light. Once the body of Light is attracted, you can move onto the next ray and anchor it into your body.

RAY X—ANCHORING OF THE BODY OF LIGHT, INVITING OF THE SOUL MERGE

The color of this ray is pearlescent. Because of the pearlescent coloring, it has all the rainbow effects within it. This ray helps one to integrate and balance their yin and yang aspects of self and realize they are one with all. I utilize this ray most of the time in healing sessions to help one balance and feel comfortable within.

RAY XI—THE BRIDGE TO THE NEW AGE

The color of this ray is Pink-Orange. This particular ray brings forth an energy of balance and calm. It helps the body wash away any other energetic matrixes that a person no longer needs. It also helps us to step more fully into the New Age of Aquarius. If an area, town, country, or person needs peace and calm in their life, call in this ray to cover the area or person, given the person has granted permission to do so.

RAY XII—ANCHORING OF THE NEW AGE AND CHRIST CONSCIOUSNESS

The color of this ray is Gold. This ray is to anchor in Christ consciousness here on Mother Earth. This is the Mother of all energies. It helps in every aspect of our lives here on earth. Utilize this ray on a daily basis in prayer and you will find yourself blessed in every way imaginable.

All of the twelve rays above utilize and encompass different qualities of energy. As you study the above rays, you can utilize their power and effectiveness in any given situation. You can choose to use these rays for yourself, or be called in service to help heal the world. However, you cannot send these rays to anyone else unless you have their permission. I believe that if you send it to the highest good for that person when they are ready, the ray could potentially help.

Here's the best part about the rays. No matter where a soul is on their evolution, each has the ability and right to call on these rays at any given opportunity. It is their God-given choice to do so. It's really simple to call forth the ray of your choice. You can do it in a combination of rays. I wouldn't do all at once. Practice calling them in one at a time to get a feel for the energy of each one.

So here's how you do it. "I call upon the 12th Golden Ray to encompass and cover the area of San Francisco for everyone's highest and best good." You can call upon the number of the ray, such as, "I call upon the second ray to provide me with love and wisdom in my relationship." Or you can call in the color of the ray, for example, "I call forth the pink orange ray to provide me with peace and balance today and every day." Be careful and use caution with the use of Ray I and IV as these rays could create havoc. Given a person's personality and negative ego, they could cause more conflict than help. It would be best to call in an ascended master to help with these two rays for the appropriateness and usefulness of these two rays. Please use good judgment and discernment. Otherwise, use your intuition in any given situation.

Another frequency of light I call upon is the Mahatma energies. These are the highest Godhead energies known to man according to Joshua Stone, PhD. The energies are very pure and high in frequency. When I call in these energies, I wash the person's chakras and vital internal organs with the light all the way through their body. When you do this, you are releasing negative energies within the body and returning the body (DNA) back into God's energy, a pure source.

When you love and respect yourself,
it shall create a domino effect
into the world.

- Mary Bannon

Mary Bannon

CHAPTER ELEVEN

Spirit Energy of Ghosts and Crossing Ghosts Over

This book about energy would not be complete unless I explain my views about the differences between ghosts and spirits on the other side. Because of my extensive experience of years of ghost hunting, I have learned the difference between the energies of ghosts and the energy of spiritual beings who are in Heaven or another term is *"on the other side."* Being clairsentient has allowed me the opportunity to feel the differences in the heaviness or lightness of the atmospheric pressure all around us. Ghosts are a lower vibrating energy whereas it feels heavier, while spirits who have crossed over to *the other side* are a much lighter energy.

Ghosts are entities who have not crossed over when they died. They chose to stay behind and not go to the light because of something they are attached to here on the earth plane, accounting for the heavier energy they carry. There are numerous reasons for this.

1) They may have stayed behind because of a loved one who was not ready for them to leave physically.

2) It could be because of something material here on earth that they are attached to such as furniture, their money, their life's work, or their home, estate, or possessions.

3) They may be scared about being judged by God.

4) Some ghosts stay behind to protect their land or their property.

5) They may have died in a traumatic accident and don't realize they are dead.

6) I encountered a ghost that stayed behind because they died while scuba diving. They refused to let go of their scuba gear because they thought they were still alive when instead, they were reliving their experience over and over again.

Ghosts who stayed behind only have a certain amount of time to decide whether to follow the tunnel of light and cross over to heaven. If they don't take this opportunity, they are stuck here in their plane of existence until they find a person who has the ability to help them cross over, if and when they are ready to do so. An intent for them to cross and be drawn over to the other side must be made for them.

Ghosts are also able to see your light that you emit if you are connected to divine energies. When you go to the grocery store and a ghost is following their respective family, they will see your beacon of light and may perhaps follow you home and hang out until you notice them and you can cross them over. Generally, I like to take time once a week to cross people over.

Ghosts will definitely let me know they are around if I don't take the time to cross them. When word gets around in the ghost community, there will be literally hundreds that come to be crossed over.

A battlefield is a place where a lot of people have been killed. You can bet there will be ghosts haunting the area, not knowing yet that they have been killed, which has been my experience. They seem to just walk around aimlessly paralyzed to the situation. The energy of battle also sticks around as when you have energy that happens over and over again, such as a cannon or guns being shot, this usually leaves an energy imprint.

In the United States, there are many battlefields because of the many wars between Native Americans long before the migration of Europeans. However, I have found not many Native American ghosts linger when we have been to their battlefields, and I believe the reason for that is they have and/or had ceremonial rituals after battles to help cross them over to The Great Spirit. Native Americans have always been and still are very spiritual beings.

However, the same does not hold true for other battles fought over literally thousands of years throughout the world. There are literally thousands of ghosts still walking around in many different countries waiting to be crossed over.

When I went on vacation in Mexico, I visited a Mayan ruin. I knew there were many ghosts there who had not yet crossed. I went behind a temple and sat down and meditated. I called in the angels and ascended masters to help. There were at least 60 ghosts standing around me, waiting to see what I was going to do. They didn't recognize the angels I brought in to help them cross because angels were not a part of their culture. They were totally confused. I immediately asked my spirit guides what I should do. They suggested that I bring in the bird Kukulkan, the great feathered serpent. That worked. They all climbed aboard the big bird and flew to Heaven. So there will be times that you have to put the scenario in terms the ghost can understand in order to cross them.

Crossing Ghosts Over to the Other Side

I'm sure there may be hundreds of ways to cross entities over to the other side; however, the following is how I do it.

Ask God to surround you in pure white light as though a lamp is turned on behind you shining down and illuminating your entire body. Next, ask God for protection of all concerned. Ask the archangels to bring someone the entity knows to come forward to help them with crossing over. Either in your head or out loud, explain to the ghost that the transition will be harmless to them and that they are loved and accepted on the other side no matter what they have done here on earth. Expand the energy of your heart and send them your love to help them feel secure and safe. Ask the ghost to step into the light with you. Once the ghost has crossed, you will feel how much lighter the room/space feels to you or perhaps you will see it happening depending on your psychic ability.

If a spirit is not ready to go yet, no worries, you can still create the intent for them that they are to be crossed over when they are ready and to allow for that to happen.

As I stated above, I cross spirits over on a weekly basis. I have created space for the ghosts to "hang out." They do not hang out in my home, however. I created space, such as a living room complete with a couch, chairs, magazines, bathroom and television on top of my roof. It is completely contained with four walls, heated, air conditioned—all the comforts of home. I have also made the statement, they are not allowed in my home itself. Their temporary home is upstairs on top of the roof in the space I created in my mind for them. This has worked great. Every Sunday I just connect with God, bring in the white light, I place myself upstairs with them (in my mind of course), and cross them over. It's now a ceremonial ritual every Sunday that I do this.

I wish you good luck on this process as it a beautiful service to help a person who has been left behind and who is a fractionated energy left here in a different plane of existence from his soul. Once the fractionated part of the soul here goes back to the soul in heaven, it helps the soul become whole once again.

Plus, you can also make the statement when working with your spirit guides, that if you have a fractionated soul that is living in a different reality or plane of existence, that they also come to your rooftop to be crossed at their divine time.

Clearing Space

After you have crossed spirits over it is always a great idea to clear your space. The following should help you with this procedure. You will want to be in your heart space and claim the space you are clearing with your heart and intent. Your intent can be as simple as this house is mine and no other energy may prevail in this home, or Lord, please fill this home with loving, high vibrational energies, or Jesus, please fill my home with your loving light. The possibilities of ceremonial prayers are endless; just keep it light, simple, and pure. The following tools can be used when clearing space:

- White sage—Burn and fan this as an incense in every room of your house or building.

- White selenite wand—Wave this in every room.

- Tibetan incense—Burn and fan this incense.

- Crystal grids—Create a crystal grid with black tourmaline or black obsidian to be placed in a room. Expand the grid's energy by placing a pyramid on top.

Now walk through every room of the home or building starting in the left corner and work your way around to the front door all the while smudging or using the white selenite wand or incense, and saying, "I bless this home/house with love and light."

Conclusion

It is with my pure intent and hopefulness that this book is received well into the community and that people talk about it with joy and happiness knowing with each soul that this book reaches, it may help them on their path of enlightenment and healing. We are all a part of this world, and it is up to us and our soul and consciousness to make it a happy place to live. Let's make positive changes for this world without hate, crime, and abusiveness and make it into a world full of hope, dreams, and faith in God.

By living and working in the medical field, I saw firsthand how when people gave up their fight with whatever illness they had; they usually succumbed to their own death within a short period of time. I worked with the AIDS population for many years, and when they gave up their fight over their disease, death didn't take long to come. When people who go to hospice, their will to survive and continue in this lifetime ceases within a few months. My point being, giving up, gives up life.

Let us fully consider healing ourselves with perfection. Using our minds and allowing our bodies to heal itself, believing that we are perfect and whole. Our minds and bodies are very intelligent. Going back to positive affirmations, let's take it one step further and believe our body to be in perfect condition as though nothing had ever happened, such as with psoriasis, high blood pressure, or cancer—changing our DNA with our minds so to speak. As you read about Masaru Emoto and changing the water crystals, or in our case, our molecules, with positive thoughts and affirmation and prayer, changing our DNA as though our illness never existed will be the new horizon for healing our bodies. A new paradigm will be created for all.

After learning about energy and working with it, you have the perfect opportunity to learn and grow from it. Being in compassion, love, and pure joy brings forth lots of happiness within yourself along with true manifesting desires and health. As the years progress, the rate of our manifesting skills will grow exponentially as more people awaken to their spirituality and start utilizing their gifts from God, our Creator.

As of this writing, all I have to do is think it and it is created— this includes health. More and more people are achieving this manifestiation skill by opening their hearts and allowing more love to flow in. Love is the key to manifesting, especially where our health is involved. It is truly a powerful spiritual journey.

May you all live in peace, love, harmony, prosperity, and balance.

References

Brennan, Barbara A., *Hands of Light*, Bantam Books, 1987.

Emoto, Masaru, *The Hidden Messages in Water,* Atria Books, 2005.

Hay, Louise, *You Can Heal Your Life,* Hay House, 1984.

Stone, Joshua David, *The Complete Ascension Manual,* Light Technology Publishing, 1994.